COLLINS

HANDY TOWN PLAN ATLAS

BRITAIN

CONTENTS

Published by Collins
An imprint of HarperCollins Publishers

77-85 Fulham Palace Road, Hammersmith, London W6 8JB
Mapping generated from Bartholomew digital databases

Copyright © HarperCollins Publishers Ltd 1999
Mapping © Bartholomew Ltd 1997, 1999

Town and city centre maps on pages 21 to 121 except pages 37 and 113 based upon the Ordnance Survey Mapping with the permission of The Controller of Her Majesty's Stationery Office © Crown copyright 399302

Printed in Italy   ISBN 0 00 448810 5   LC9835   BNA
e-mail: roadcheck@harpercollins.co.uk
web site: www.bartholomewmaps.com

HarperCollins*Publishers*

Broad Haven
Templeton
Narberth
A4076
A477
Milford Haven
Johnston
Saunders-
foot
A477
Kidwelly
(Cydwelli)
A4066
A476
Skomer
Island
Neyland
A477
Tenby
Kidwelly
(Cydwelli)
Pembrey
Burry Port
S
Pembroke
Dock
Pembroke
Carmarthen
Bay
SWAN
S
To Rosslare
A4139
Manorbier
Caldey Island
Llanrhidian
A4118
St Govan's Head
Worms Head
Mum

To Cork
B
r

Isles of Scilly

Hugh Town

Ilfracombe
A3·99
A431

Lundy
Island

Croyde
A361

Barnstaple
or
Bideford Bay
Braunton
Fremington
Appledor
Hartland Point
Westward Ho!
A39
Bideford

Hartland
Great

Stibb Cross
A386

Kilkhampton
A·388

16 miles to 1 inch
0   10   20 miles
0   10   20   30 km
10 km to 1 cm

Bude
Stratton
A3072
Highampton
Holsworthy
A3079
Okehamp

Bude
Bay
A39
Wainhouse Corner
Tamar
A30
Lydford
A386

Tintagel
Hallworthy
Launceston
A395
A30
Lydford
A386

Delabole
Camelford
Tavistock

St Endellion
B o d m i n   M o o r
A388

Padstow
C O R N W A L L
Callington
Ho

Wadebridge
A390
St Ive
A388
P

Trenance
A39
Bodmin
Liskeard
A386

Newquay
A3059
St Columb
Major
A30
A38
A38
Saltash

A392
Lostwithiel
A390
Torpoint
Ply

Perranporth
A391
Par
Sandplace
East
Looe
Plymsto

St Agnes
Goonhavern
A3058
St Austell
Polperro

Portreath
A390
Probus
Mevagissey

St Ives
Redruth
Truro
Tregony

Zennor
A30
Camborne
A39

Pendeen
Hayle
Penryn
St Mawes

St Just
A3071
Marazion
A394
Falmouth

A30
Penzance
A394
Helston

Land's End
Sennen
St Keverne

Mount's Bay
A3083

Lizard Point
Lizard

To Santander (summer only)
To Roscoff

SUFFOLK

Fordham · Burwell · A143 · Ixworth · A140 · Westleton
A10 · Newmarket · Bury St Edmunds · Debenham · Framlingham · Saxmundham · Leiston
A14 · Stradishall · Stowmarket · Needham Market · Wickham Market · A12 · A1094 · Tunstall · Aldeburgh
Great Shelford · Sawston · A11 · A1037 · Lavenham · Long Melford · Claydon · Woodbridge · Orford
Haverhill · Sudbury · **Ipswich** · Hadleigh · A14 · A14
M11 · Saffron Walden · A1092 · A1071 · A12 · **Felixstowe**
Newport · Sible Hedingham · Halstead · Manningtree · Harwich
Thaxted · Gosfield · A131 · A134 · Stour · A120 · **Harwich**

ESSEX

Stansted Mountfitchet · Stansted ✈ · Braintree · Coggeshall · Wivenhoe · Walton-on-Naze · Frinton-on-Sea
Bishop's Stortford · Great Dunmow · A120 · **Colchester** · Brightlingsea · A133 · Holland-on-Sea · Clacton-on-Sea
n City · A130 · A131 · Kelvedon · Tiptree · West Mersea
Harlow · A106 · Witham · Tollesbury · Blackwater
oddesdon · A414 · **Chelmsford** · Maldon · Bradwell Waterside
eshunt · Chipping Ongar · A414 · Southminster
M11 · Ingatestone · A130 · South Woodham Ferrers · Burnham-on-Crouch
Brentwood · **Billericay** · Crouch
Romford · Wickford · Rayleigh · Rochford
A12 · A127 · **Basildon** · **SOUTHEND**
Ilford · A13 · M25 · **Southend-on-Sea**
London City · THURROCK · A13 · Canvey Island
Grays · Tilbury · River Thames · Sheerness
Dartford · **Gravesend** · Isle of Sheppey · Queenborough · **Margate** · North Foreland
mley · A2 · Rochester · **Gillingham** · Herne Bay · **Broadstairs**
pington · A20 · **Chatham** · A249 · Whitstable · A253 · **Ramsgate**
A21 · M20 · Sittingbourne · Faversham · A28 · Sandwich
M26 · West Malling · A228 · A249 · M2 · Sturry · A257 · **Deal**
S · A25 · **Maidstone** · A2 · **Canterbury** · A256
Oxted · Sevenoaks · A26 · **North** · **Downs** · Chilham · A28 · Temple Ewell
Tonbridge · Headcorn · Ashford · A28 · **Dover**
Southborough · Pembury · Staplehurst · Sellindge · A28 · **Folkestone**
Royal Tunbridge Wells · A21 · A229 · Kingsnorth · A2070 · Hythe · Channel tunnel
East Grinstead · The Weald · Hawkhurst · Tenterden · Hamstreet · Dymchurch
Crowborough · Hurst Green · Four Oaks · A259 · New Romney
A26 · Maresfield · Burwash · Dungeness
A272 · Uckfield · Heathfield · A21 · Icklesham · Rye
EAST SUSSEX · Battle · Westfield
s Hill · Herstmonceux · Hollington · A259
Lewes · Beddingham · Hailsham · **Hastings**
Polegate · Bexhill
ghton · A27 · Willingdon · Pevensey
acehaven · Seaford · **Eastbourne** · Beachy Head

To Göteborg · To Esbjerg · To Hamburg · To Hoek van Holland · To Dunkerque

Strait of Dover · Channel tunnel

Calais

Boulogne-sur-Mer

C H A N N E L

To Dieppe

16 miles to 1 inch
0 · 10 · 20 miles
0 · 10 · 20 · 30 km
10 km to 1 cm

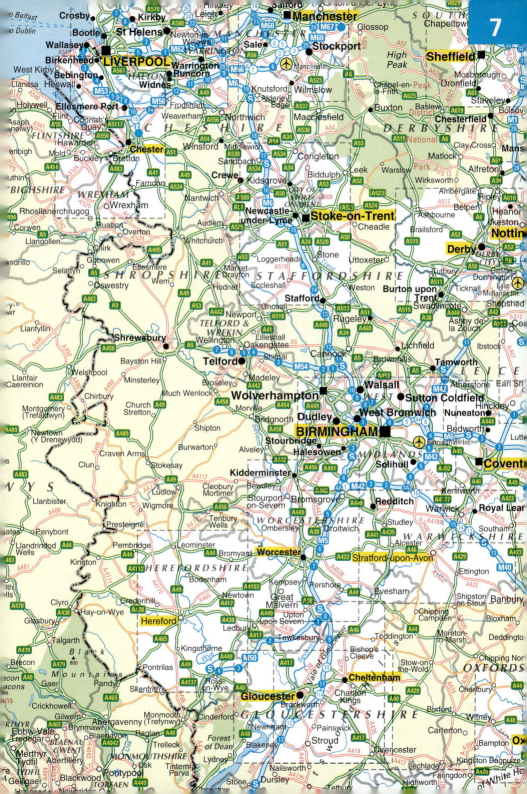

16 miles to 1 inch

0   10   20 miles

0   10   20   30 km

10 km to 1 cm

ton

e Head

LNSHIRE

To Rotterdam & Zeebrugge

ercotes

Mablethorpe

Maltby le Marsh

lford

ey Ingoldmells

A158

y Burgh
le Marsh Skegness

Wainfleet
All Saints

A52

angle

*Blakeney
Point*

Brancaster Blakeney Sheringham

The Hunstanton Wells-next- Cromer
the-Sea

Wash Heacham Holt **A148** Mundesley

Snettisham Docking North Happisburgh
Walsham **A149**

Fakenham Aylsham Stalham
Dersingham **A148** Guist Cawston **A140** Coltishall Hemsby

King's South Wootton **A1065** Bawdeswell Hoveton *The* Caister-on-Sea
Lynn Norwich **A1062**
A17 **NORFOLK** East Acle **Great
A47** Dereham **A47** Sprowston *Broads* **A47** **Yarmouth**
A47 Narborough Necton **Norwich** **A12**
A10 Swaffham **A11** Loddon **A143** Hopton
Wisbech **A1065** Watton Wymondham Corton
A1122 Stradsett Brooke Haddiscoe **A1117** Oulton
A1101 Downham **A134** Attleborough **A140** Beccles **A146** **Lowestoft**
Market Long Bungay
Southery Mundford **A11** Larling Stratton **A143** Kessingland
Methwold **A1065** **A134** Homersfield **A12**
Littleport Brandon Harleston Brampton
SHIRE Lakenheath Thetford **A1066** Diss Halesworth
Ely **A11** Scole Southwold
A142 **A143** **A1120**
Stretham Mildenhall Eye
123 Icklingham Stanton Westleton
Burwell Fordham **A14** Ixworth **A140** Saxmundham
A10 Bury St Edmunds Debenham Leiston

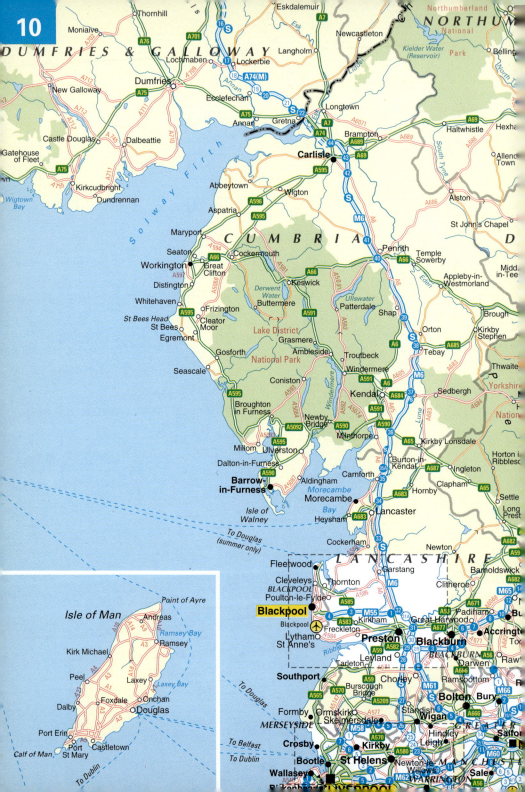

RLAND
Ashington
Newbiggin-by-the-Sea
Morpeth
A197
A189
To Bergen, Haugesund & Stavanger
Blyth
Bedlington
Cramlington
To Göteborg (summer only)
Ponteland
A19
Whitley Bay
North Shields
Tynemouth
A696
Newcastle
Gosforth
A69
South Shields
A1
Newcastle upon Tyne
Gateshead
A1018
TYNE AND WEAR
A194(M)
A1
A19
Sunderland
A68
Stanley
A692
A693
A1018
bridge
A695
Corsett
A167
Chester-le-Street
Houghton le Spring
A691
Durham
62
Easington
A167
Peterlee
Wear
olsingham
Crook
Spennymoor
A181
Hartlepool
HARTLEPOOL
HAM
A688
A1(M)
A173
A19
A689
Bishop Auckland
A68
Shildon
Aycliffe
A689
Billingham
A085
Redcar
REDCAR AND CLEVELAND
Brotton
Middlesbrough
A688
South Bank
Stockton-on-Tees
A66
MIDDLESBROUGH
Hinderwell
Barnard Castle
DARLINGTON
Guisborough
A174
Sandsend
Winston
Darlington
Teesside Int.
Thornaby-on-Tees
Whitby
Bowes
A66
57
Stokesley
A171
Gilling West
Scotch Corner
Stokesley
Sleights
Richmond
A684
A172
Robin Hood's Bay
A1
Catterick
North York Moors
A171
Northallerton
A19
North York Moors National Park
Burniston
Leyburn
A684
Leeming
A168
A169
Scalby
A170
Scarborough
Aysgarth
Bedale
Kirkbymoorside
Eastfield
Middleham
A1
Thirsk
A170
Helmsley
Pickering
Snainton
Filey
Masham
A61
Oswaldkirk
Vale of Pickering
A1039
Hunmanbyo
A64
Kettlewell
A6108
Topcliffe
Malton
Norton
Flamborough
Ripon
A19
Easingwold
North Grimston
Flamborou
Pateley Bridge
A168
Boroughbridge
Stillington
Langtoft
A614
A165
Bridlington
Grassington
A61
Ripley
A1(M)
Haxby
A64
Bridlington Bay
Hetton
Knaresborough
Fridaythorpe
Great Driffield
Skipsea
Skipton
A59
Harrogate
A658
A61
York
A166
EAST RIDING OF YORKSHIRE
Ilkley
A65
Spofforth
Wetherby
A1237
Fulford
Stamford Bridge
Pocklington
Brandesburton
Hornsea
Steeton
A660
A658
Boston Spa
YORK
A1079
Bainton
Otley
A61
A58
Tadcaster
A64
Hayton
Market Weighton
A1079
A1035
A165
South Skirlaugh
Aldbrough
Keighley
Birstall
A64
A19
Holme-on-Spalding-Moor
A614
A1034
Leven
Bradford
Pudsey
A642
Garforth
Bubwith
A163
CITY OF KINGSTON UPON HULL
Bilton
Queensbury
M621
Leeds
A1
Selby
North Cave
A63
South Cave
A164
Anlaby
A63
Kingston upon Hull
A646
Halifax
Castleford
A1041
Goole
M62
A1033
Patrington
Dewsbury
A644
Wakefield
Pontefract
Knottingley
Snaith
A161
NORTH LINCOLNSHIRE
Barton-upon-Humber
A15
M62
Huddersfield
A638
A628
Thorne
Crowle
Winterton
A1077
A160
Mouth of The Hu
Immingham
Grimsby
M1
Barnsley
South Kirkby
Hatfield
Bentley
M18
M180
M181
Scunthorpe
Bottesford
Humberside Int.
Holmfirth
A628
Wombwell
A635
Doncaster
Epworth
A15
Caistor
A46
Oldham
A629
Mexborough
A614
A161
A159
Ashton-under-Lyne
SOUTH YORKSHIRE
Blyton
A1103
chester
Chapeltown
Rotherham
A1(M)
A631
Gainsborough
Market Rasen
M67
Glossop
A61
M18
Maltby
A631
A156
tockport
High
Sheffield
A57

16 miles to 1 inch
10 miles
20 miles
10 km to 1 cm
30 km

To IJmuiden & Hamburg (summer only)

N O R T H   S E A

Dundee
Broughty Ferry
Tayport
New Scone
Perth
Newburgh
Leuchars
St Andrews
Cupar
Pitscottie
Auchtermuchty
Ladybank
Fife Ness
F I F E
Falkland
Crail
Kinross
Markinch
Anstruther
Pittenweem
Glenrothes
Leven
Elie
Buchhaven
Largo Bay
Lochgelly
Kirkcaldy
Burntisland
North Berwick
Dunfermline
Gullane
Inverkeithing
Cockenzie and Port Seton
East Linton
Dunbar
CITY OF EDINBURGH
Leith
Musselburgh
Prestonpans
Haddington
Cockburnspath
St Abb's Head
Edinburgh
Dalkeith
Gifford
Coldingham
Eyemouth
Bonnyrigg
Humbie
EAST LOTHIAN
MIDLOTHIAN
Gorebridge
Chirnside
Berwick-upon-Tweed
Penicuik
Lammermuir Hills
Duns
Tweedmouth
West Linton
Swinton
Moorfoot Hills
Lauder
Greenlaw
Holy Island or Lindisfarne
Blyth Bridge
Stow
Gordon
Coldstream
Farne Islands
Peebles
Galashiels
Earlston
Flodden
Bamburgh
Biggar
Innerleithen
Melrose
Kelso
Belford
North Sunderland
Tweed
SCOTTISH
Selkirk
Newtown St Boswells
Kilham
Wooler
Hawick
Jedburgh
Morebattle
Glanton
Alnwick
Longhoughton
B O R D E R S
Teviotdale
Bonchester Bridge
Cheviot Hills
Rothbury
Warkworth
Amble
Moffat
Beattock
Eskdalemuir
Northumberland National Park
Otterburn
Ashington
Newbiggin-by-the-Sea
Newcastleton
N O R T H U M B E R L A N D
Morpeth
Blyth
Langholm
Kielder Water (Reservoir)
Bellingham
Bedlington
Cramlington
Lockerbie
Ponteland
Newcastle
North Shields
Whit
Tyr
Ecclefechan
Longtown
Corbridge
Gosforth
So
Annan
Gretna
Brampton
Haltwhistle
Hexham
Newcastle upon Tyne
Gateshead
Carlisle
Allendale Town
Stanley
Chester-le-Hou
Consett
Durham
Peterle
Abbeytown
Wigton
Alston
Wolsingham
Crook
Aspatria
St John's Chapel
Spennymoor
C U M B R I A
D U R H A M
Cockermouth
Penrith
Temple Sowerby
Bishop Auckland
Shildon
Middles

16 miles to 1 inch
10 km to 1 cm

(Rhum)
Eigg
Muck
Morar
Arisaig
A830
Glenfinnan
A830
A82
Spean Bridge
Oban to Lochboisdale
Sound of Arisaig
A861
Loch Shiel
A861
A82
Fort William
Ben Nevis
1344
Loch Arkaig

Oban to Castlebay

Coll
Kilchoan
Salen
Strontian
A861
A884
Kinlochle
Ballachulish
Glen Coe
A82
1150
Bidean
Nam Bian
A82

Tiree
Tobermory
A848
Lochaline
Loch Linnhe
Portnacroish
A828
Bridge of Orc

Salen
Ulva
Lismore
A828
Loch Etive
Glen Orch

M u l l
Ben More
966
Craignure
A849
A85
A85
Oban
Taynuilt
Dalmally
A85

Iona
Fionnphort
Pennyghael
A849
A R G Y L L
Loch Awe
A N D B U T E
A816
A819
Clachan
A83
Arroc
Loch

Firth of Lorn
Luing
Kilmelford
Argyll
A815
A816
Ga
Helen

Colonsay
Scalasaig
Scarba
Kilmartin
A83
A886
A815
A816
A806

Oronsay
Jura
Tarbert
Lochgilphead
Tayvallich
Ardrishaig
A83
Kilfinan
Auchenbreck
Gre
Dunoon
Gourock
Port Gla
INV
Wem
Bay

Port Askaig
A846
Tarbert
A83
A886
Rothesay
Bute
Larg
A78
Millport
NOR
AYRS
Wes
Kilbr
A78

I s l a y
A846
Bowmore
A846
To Scalasaig &
Port Ellen
A83
Claonaig
Sound of Bute
A841
Lochranza
A841
Ardrossan
Saltcoats
A78

Portnahaven
A847
Loch Indaal
Gigha
Tayinloan
A841
Brodick

Port Ellen
Mull Of Oa
Carradale
Kilbrannan Sound
Arran
Lamlash

16 miles to 1 inch
0   10   20 miles
0   10   20   30 km
10 km to 1 cm
A83
Machrihanish
Campbeltown
Lagg
Firth of Clyde

Kintyre
Southend

Rathlin
Island
Mull of Kintyre
To Ballycastle
Turnberry
Ailsa Craig
Girvan
S
A
Y

Portrush
Portstewart
A2
A2
Bushmills
Bush
A44
Ballycastle
A2
Cushendun
A77
Coleraine
A26
Armoy
Cushendun
Colmonell

Rubha Robhanais
Port Nis
A857
Barabhas
Tolsta Head
Carlabhagh
A858
Miavaig
Great Bernera
Gearraidh na h-Aibhne
Stornoway (Steornabhagh)
Loch a' Tuath
Port nan Giúran
Loch Langavat
A859
Lewis (Eilean Leodhais)
Scarp
Kebock Head
Ullapool to Stornoway
The Minch
Sur

WESTERN ISLES (NA H-EILEANAN AN IAR)

An Tairbeart
A859
Scalpay (Eilean Scalpaigh)
Shiant Islands
Rubha Reidh
Loch Tarbert
South Harris
Taobh Tuath
Pabbay
Roghadal
Rubha Hunish
Poolewe
Gairloch
Sound of Harris
Kilmaluag
Baile Mhartainn
A865
North Uist (Uibhist a' Tuath)
A865 A867
Lochmaddy (Loch na Madadh)
Uig
A855
Sound of Raas
Rona
Shieldaig
To
Heisker or Monach Islands
Loch Snizort
A87
719
Little Minch
Benbecula (Beinn na Faoghla)
Loch Dunvegan
A850
Dunvegan
Borve
A896
Inner Sound
Raasay
Portree
Lochcarro
Loch Bracadale
Skye
Bracadale
A863
South Uist (Uibhist a' Deas)
Scalpay
Sligachan
A87
Kyle of Lochalsh
A87
Lochboisdale (Loch Baghasdail)
Cuillin Hills
Broadford
Kyleakin
(summer only)
928
Blaven (Bla Bheinn)
Eriskay (Eiriosgaigh)
Soay
Elgol
Loch Eishort
Canna
Loch Hourn
Ardvasar
Sound of Sleat
Knoydart
Barra (Eilean Barraigh)
Rum (Rhum)
Mallaig
A851
Loch Nevis
Vatersay (Bhatarsaigh)
Castlebay (Bagh a' Chaisteil)
Morar
Loch Morar
Pabaigh
Eigg
Arisaig
A830
Oban to Lochboisdale
Muck
Sound of Arisaig
A861
Mingulay (Miughalaigh)
Oban to Castlebay
Loch Shiel

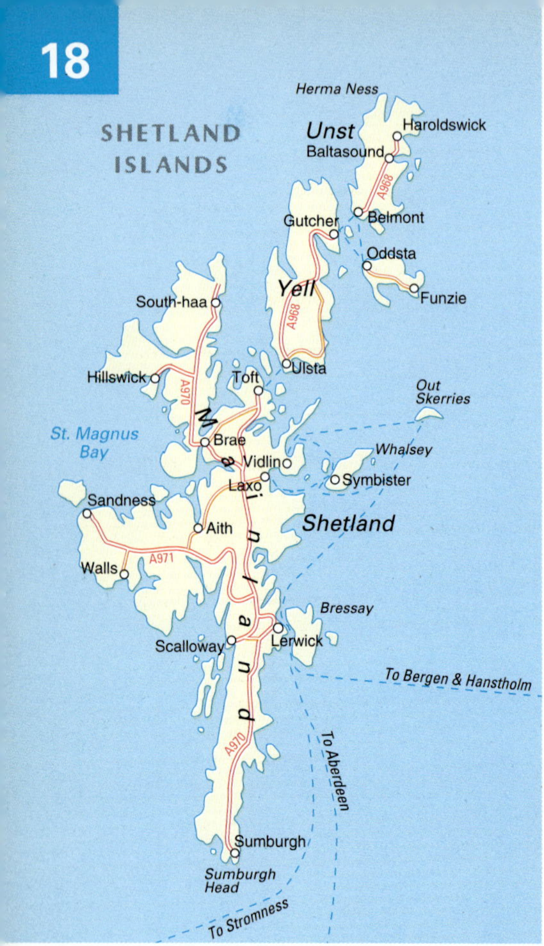

SHETLAND ISLANDS
Herma Ness
Unst
Haroldswick
Baltasound
A968
Gutcher
Belmont
Oddsta
Yell
A968
Funzie
South-haa
Ulsta
Hillswick
A970
Toft
Out Skerries
St. Magnus Bay
Brae
Mainland
Vidlin
Whalsey
Laxo
Symbister
Sandness
Aith
Shetland
Walls
A971
Bressay
Scalloway
Lerwick
To Bergen & Hanstholm
To Aberdeen
A970
Sumburgh
Sumburgh Head
To Stromness

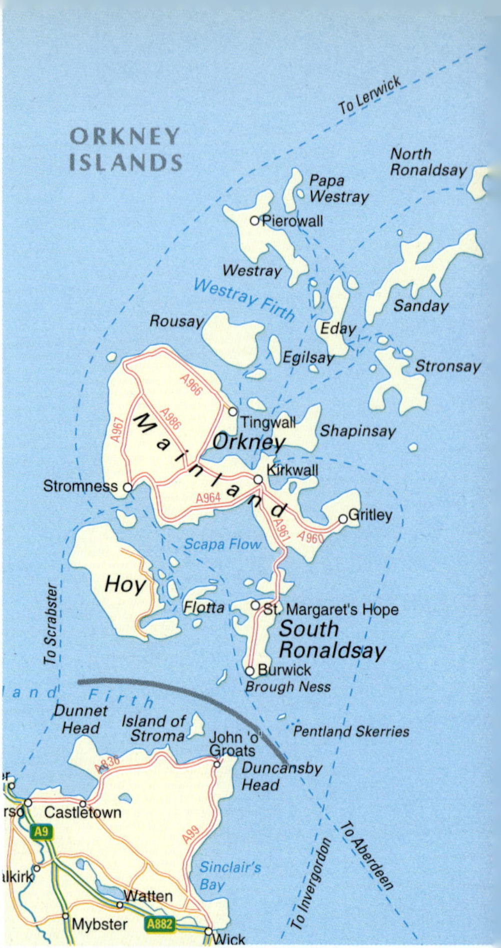

ORKNEY ISLANDS
To Lerwick
North Ronaldsay
Papa Westray
Pierowall
Westray
Westray Firth
Sanday
Rousay
Eday
Egilsay
Stronsay
A966
A986
A967
Tingwall
Shapinsay
Mainland
Orkney
Kirkwall
Stromness
A964
A961
A960
Gritley
Scapa Flow
Hoy
To Scrabster
Flotta
St. Margaret's Hope
South Ronaldsay
Burwick
Brough Ness
Pentland Firth
Dunnet Head
Island of Stroma
John 'o' Groats
Pentland Skerries
Duncansby Head
A836
Castletown
A9
A99
Sinclair's Bay
To Invergordon
To Aberdeen
Watten
Mybster
A882
Wick

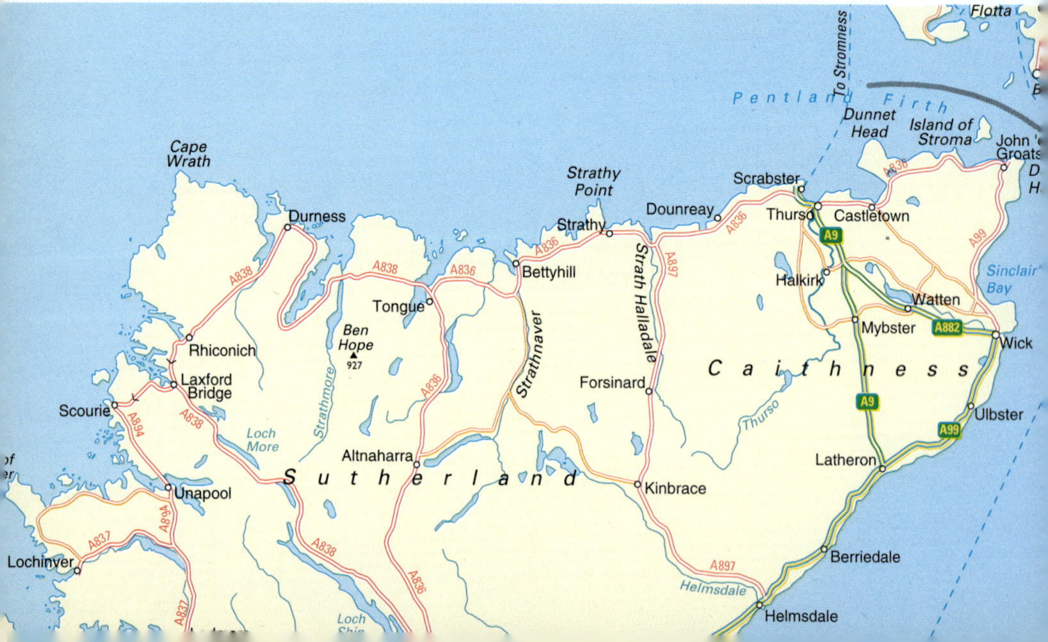

Flotta
To Stromness
Pentland Firth
Dunnet Head
Island of Stroma
Cape Wrath
Strathy Point
Scrabster
Durness
Dounreay
Thurso
Castletown
Strathy
A836
A838
A836
A838
A836
A9
A99
Bettyhill
Strath Halladale
A897
Halkirk
Sinclair Bay
Tongue
Watten
Ben Hope
927
Mybster
A882
Wick
Rhiconich
Strathnaver
Laxford Bridge
Forsinard
Caithness
Scourie
A894
A838
Strathmore
A836
Thurso
A9
Ulbster
Loch More
A99
Altnaharra
Latheron
Sutherland
Unapool
Kinbrace
A894
A837
A838
A836
Berriedale
Lochinver
A897
Helmsdale
Helmsdale
A837
Loch

Key to Approach Map Symbols

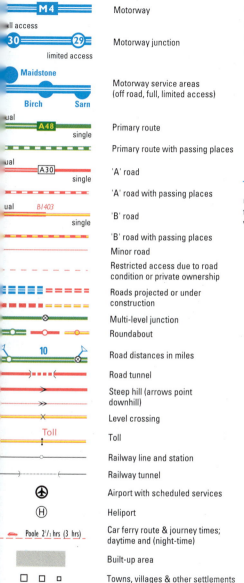

M4 full access	Motorway
30 **29** limited access	Motorway junction
Maidstone **Birch** **Sarn**	Motorway service areas (off road, full, limited access)
dual **A48** single	Primary route
dual single	Primary route with passing places
dual **A30** single	'A' road
dual single	'A' road with passing places
dual **B1403** single	'B' road
	'B' road with passing places
	Minor road
	Restricted access due to road condition or private ownership
	Roads projected or under construction
⊗	Multi-level junction
	Roundabout
10 ⊗	Road distances in miles
	Road tunnel
>	Steep hill (arrows point downhill)
×	Level crossing
Toll	Toll
	Railway line and station
	Railway tunnel
✈	Airport with scheduled services
Ⓗ	Heliport
Poole 2½ hrs (3 hrs)	Car ferry route & journey times; daytime and (night-time)
	Built-up area
□ □ ▫	Towns, villages & other settlements

	National boundary
	County / Unitary Authority boundary
	Forest park boundary
	National / Regional park boundary
	Woodland
Danger Zone	Military range
468 ▲941	Spot height / Summit height in metres
	Beach
	Lake, dam & river
	Canal / Dry canal / Canal tunnel

Check with the local tourist information office for facilities and opening times before visiting. Proposed millennium sites are shown as red and yellow symbols of the relevant category e.g. ★ or 🦖

i |i|	Tourist information office (open all year / open seasonally)
⚱	Major sports venue
🎡	Theme Park
⚔1738	Battlefield
✝	Ecclesiastical building
🏰	Castle
🏛	Historic house (with or without garden)
✿	Garden
🏛	Museum / Art Gallery
++•++	Preserved railway
Ⓜ	Ancient monument
	Motor racing circuit
	Racecourse
	Country park
	Nature reserve
	Wildlife park or Zoo
★	Other interesting feature
⛳	Golf course
(NT)	National Trust property
(NTS)	National Trust for Scotland

Key to Town Plan Symbols

	Through routes
	Restricted access
	Pedestrian precinct
	Public building
	Other important building
P P	Multi-storey / Off-street parking

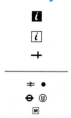

i	Tourist information office (open all year)
|i|	Tourist information office (open seasonally)
+	Ecclesiastical building
	Railway line
⇌ ●	Railway / Light Rail station
⊖ Ⓤ	Underground station
Ⓜ	Metro station (Newcastle)

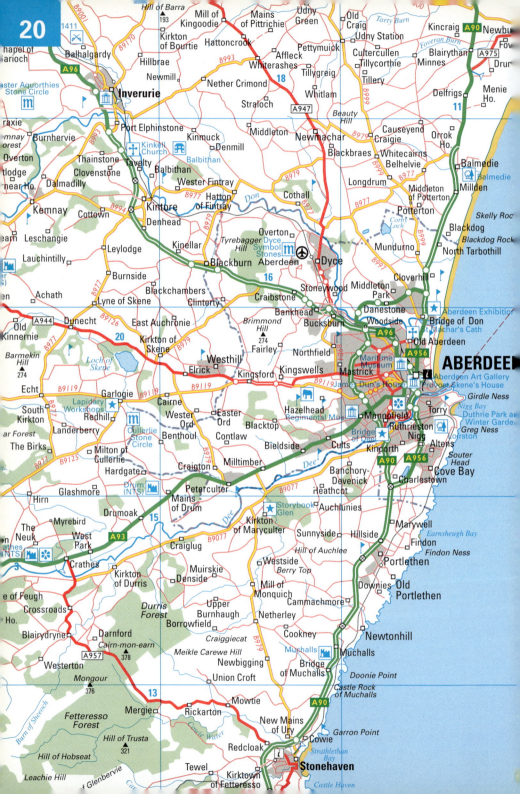

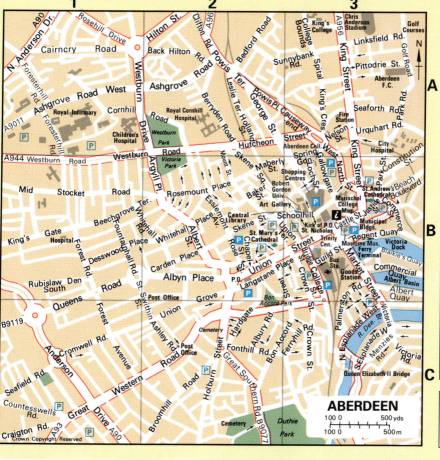

ABERDEEN

BBC RADIO ABERDEEN 990 AM
NORTHSOUND ONE 96.9 FM, NORTHSOUND TWO 1035 AM

LOCAL RADIO

STD Code 01224

ABERDEEN

TOURIST INFORMATION ☎ 01224 632727
ST. NICHOLAS HOUSE, BROAD STREET,
ABERDEEN, AB9 1DE

HOSPITAL A & E ☎ 01224 681818
ABERDEEN ROYAL INFIRMARY, FORESTERHILL,
ABERDEEN, AB25 2ZN

COUNCIL OFFICE ☎ 01224 522000
TOWN HOUSE, BROAD STREET,
ABERDEEN, AB10 1FY

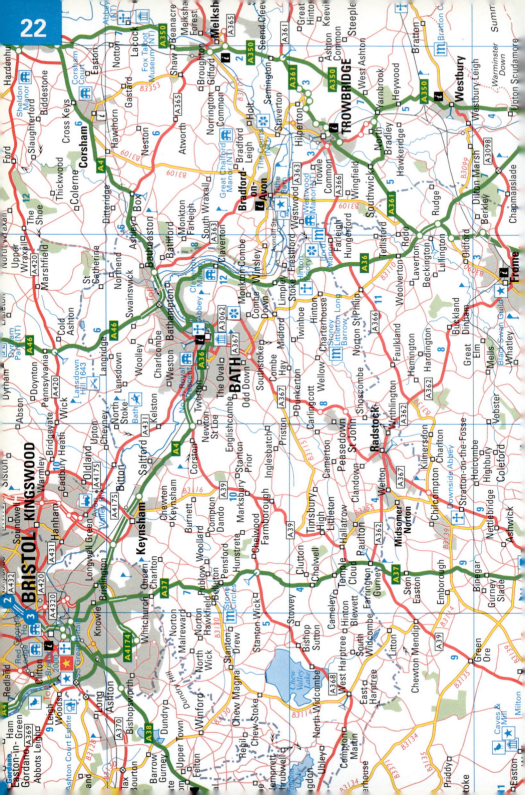

STD Code 01225

Bath and N.E. Somerset

BATH

Ambury	C2	Manvers Street	C2
Argyle Street	B2	Milk Street	B2
Avon Street	C1	Milsom Street	C1
Barton Street	B2	Monmouth Place	B2
Bath Street	B2	Monmouth Street	B2
Beau Street	B2	Newark Street	B2
Bridge Street	B2	New Bond Street	B2
Broad Quay	C2	New King Street	A2
Broad Street	A2	New Orchard Street	C2
Brock Street	A1	New Street	A1
Chapel Row	A1	North Parade	B2
Charles Street	B1	North Parade Road	B3
Charlotte Street	A1	Old King Street	A1
Cheap Street	B2	Orange Grove	B2
Claverton Street	C2	Paragon	A2
Corn Street	C1	Pierrepont Street	B2
Darlington Street	A3	Pulteney Bridge	A3
Dorchester Street	B2	Pulteney Road	C2
Gay Street	A2	Queen Street	A1
George Street	A1	Quiet Street	A1
Grand Parade	B2	Rossiter Road	B2
Great Pulteney Street	A3	St. James's Parade	A3
Green Park Road	A1	St. John's Road	C1
Grove Street	A2	Sawclose	A2
Henrietta Mews	A3	Southgate Street	B1
Henrietta Road	A3	Stall Street	B2
Henrietta Street	A3	Sydney Place	C2
Henry Street	B2	The Circus	A3
High Street	B2	Union Street	B2
Hot Bath Street	B2	Upper Borough Walls	B2
James Street West	A1	Walcot Street	B1
John Street	A2	Wells Road	C1
Kingsmead East	C1	Westgate Buildings	A1
Laura Place	A2	Westgate Street	C1
Lower Borough Walls	B2	Wood Street	A2
Lower Bristol Road	C1	York Street	B2

TOURIST INFORMATION ☎ 01225 477101
ABBEY CHAMBERS, ABBEY CHURCH YARD,
BATH, BA1 1LY

HOSPITAL A & E ☎ 01225 428331
ROYAL UNITED HOSPITAL, COMBE PARK,
BATH, BA1 3NG

COUNCIL OFFICE ☎ 01225 477000
THE GUILDHALL, HIGH STREET,
BATH, BA1 5AW

LOCAL RADIO
BBC RADIO BRISTOL 104.6 FM
GWR FM 103 FM

STD Code 0121

West Midlands

BIRMINGHAM

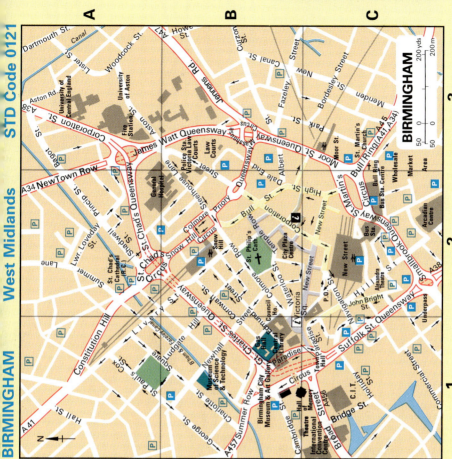

LOCAL RADIO

BBC RADIO WM 95.6 FM
XTRA AM 1152 AM, RADIO XL 1296 AM, BRMB 96.4 FM, HEART FM 100.7 FM

Albert Street	B2	Lower Loveday Street	A2
Aston Road	A3	Lower New Street	C2
Aston Street	A3	Ludgate Hill	B1
Bagot Street	A3	Masshouse Circus	B3
Bordesley Street	C3	Meriden Street	C3
Bridge Street	C1	Moor Street	C3
Broad Street	C1	Queensway	C1
Bull Ring	C3	Navigation Street	C3
Bull Street	B2	New Canal Street	B3
Cambridge Street	B1	New Town Row	A2
Charlotte Street	B1	Newhall Street	B1
Colmore Circus	B2	Paradise Circus	B1
Colmore Row	B2	Paradise Street	C1
Commercial Street	C1	Park Street	C3
Constitution Hill	A1	Princip Street	A2
Cornwall Street	B2	Priory Queensway	B2
Corporation Street	B2	Queensway	B2
Cox Street	A1	Shadwell Street	A2
Curzon Street	B3	Smallbrook	C2
Dale End		Queensway	
Dartmouth Street	A3	Snow Hill	B2
Edmund Street	B1	St. Chad's Circus	A2
Fazeley Street	B3	St. Chad's Queensway	C2
George Street	B1	St. Martin's Circus	C2
Great Charles Street	B1	St. Paul's Square	A1
Hall Street	A1	Steelhouse Lane	B2
High Street	C2	Suffolk Street	C1
Hill Street	C2	Queensway	
Holliday Street	C1	Summer Lane	A2
Howe Street	B3	Summer Row	B1
James Watt	A3	Temple Row	B2
Queensway		Upper New Street	C2
Jennens Road	B3	Victoria Square	C2
John Bright Street	C2	Waterloo Street	B2
Lister Street	A3	Woodcock Street	A3
Livery Street	A1		

TOURIST INFORMATION ☎ 0121 643 2514
2 CITY ARCADE, BIRMINGHAM,
WEST MIDLANDS, B2 4TX

HOSPITAL A & E ☎ 0121 554 3801
CITY HOSPITAL, DUDLEY ROAD,
BIRMINGHAM, B18 7QH

COUNCIL OFFICE ☎ 0121 303 9944
COUNCIL HOUSE, VICTORIA SQUARE,
BIRMINGHAM, B1 1BB

STD Code 01253

BLACKPOOL

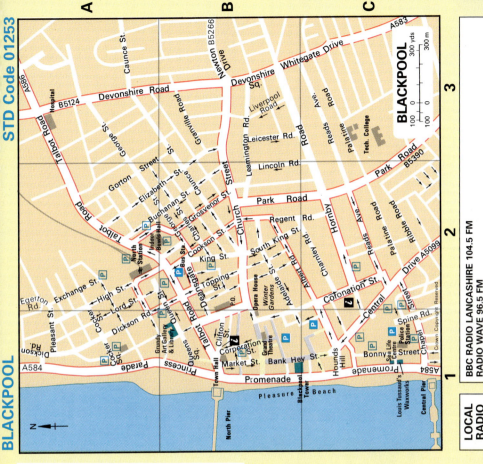

BLACKPOOL

TOURIST INFORMATION ☎ 01253 478222
1 CLIFTON STREET, BLACKPOOL, FY1 1LY

HOSPITAL A & E ☎ 01253 300000
VICTORIA HOSPITAL, WHINNEY HEYS ROAD,
BLACKPOOL, FY3 8NR

COUNCIL OFFICE ☎ 01253 477477
MUNICIPAL BUILDINGS, TOWN HALL,
CORPORATION STREET, BLACKPOOL, FY1 1AD

STD Code 01202

BOURNEMOUTH

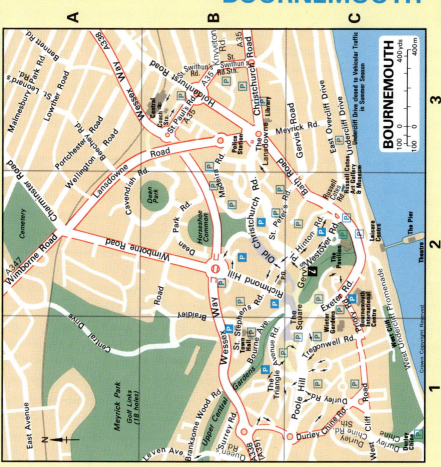

Avenue Road	B1	Malmesbury Park		
Bath Road	C2	Road	A3	
Beechey Road	A3	Meyrick Road	B3	
Bennett Road	A3	Old Christchurch Road	B2	
Bourne Avenue	B1	Poole Hill	A3	
Braidley Road	B2	Portchester Road	A3	
Branksome Wood	B1	Priory Road	C1	
Road		Queen's Road	B1	
Cavendish Road	A2	Richmond Hill	B2	
Central Drive	A1	Russell Cotes Road	C2	
Charminster Road	A2	St. Leonard's Road	A3	
Christchurch Road	B3	St. Pauls' Road	B3	
Dean Park Road	B2	St. Peter's Road	B2	
Durley Chine	C1	St. Stephen's Road	C1	
Durley Chine Road	C1	St. Swithun's Road	B3	
Durley Chine Road	C1	St. Swithun's Road	B3	
South		South		
Durley Road	C1	Surrey Road	B1	
East Avenue	A1	The Lansdowne	B3	
East Overcliff Drive	C3	The Square	C2	
Exeter Road	C2	The Triangle	B1	
Gervis Place	C2	Tregonwell Road	C2	
Gervis Road	C3	Undercliff Drive	C3	
Hinton Road	C2	Wellington Road	A2	
Holdenhurst Road	B3	Wessex Way	B1	
Knyveton Road	B3	West Cliff Road	C1	
Lansdowne Road	A2	West Undercliff	C1	
Leven Avenue	A1	Westover Road	C2	
Lowther Road	A3	Wimborne Road	A2	
Madeira Road	B2			

TOURIST INFORMATION ☎ 01202 451700
WESTOVER ROAD, BOURNEMOUTH,
DORSET, BH1 2BU

HOSPITAL A & E ☎ 01202 303626
ROYAL BOURNEMOUTH GENERAL HOSPITAL,
CASTLE LANE EAST, BOURNEMOUTH, BH7 7DW

COUNCIL OFFICE ☎ 01202 451451
TOWN HALL, BOURNE AVENUE,
BOURNEMOUTH, BH2 6DY

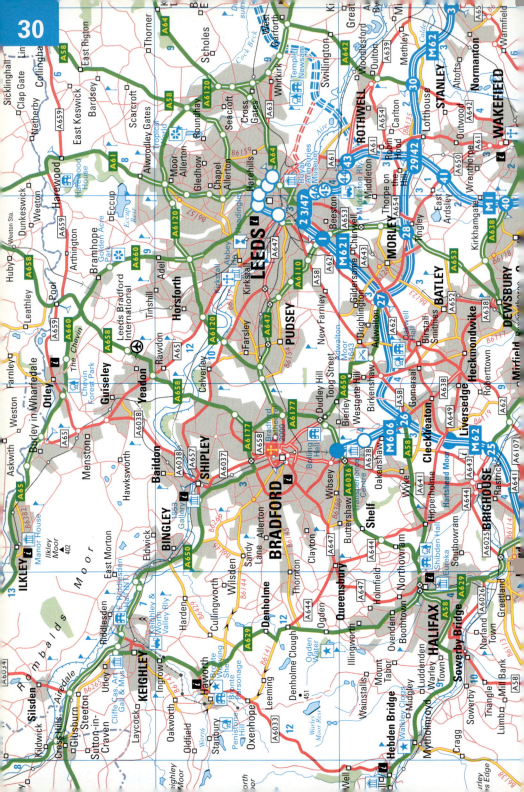

STD Code 01274   West Yorkshire   BRADFORD

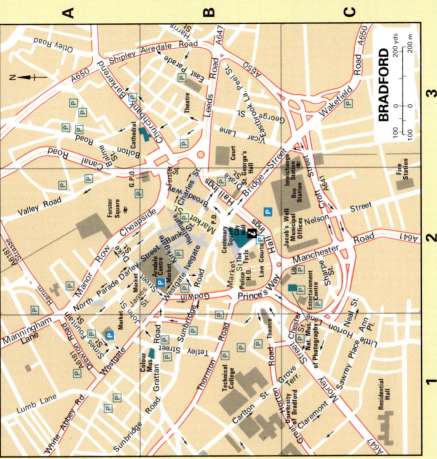

BRADFORD

LOCAL RADIO

BBC RADIO LEEDS 102.7 FM
GREAT YORKSHIRE GOLD 1278 AM, THE PULSE 97.5 FM, SUNRISE FM 103.2 FM

Ann Place	C1	Hustlergate	B2
Balme Street	A3	Ivegate	B2
Bank Street	B2	James Street	A2
Barkerend Road	A3	John Street	A1
Bolton Road	A3	Kirkgate	B2
Bridge Street	B2	Leeds Road	B3
Broadway	B2	Little Horton Lane	C1
Canal Road	A3	Lumb Lane	A1
Carlton Street	B1	Manchester Road	C2
Charles Street	B2	Manningham Lane	A1
Cheapside	A2	Manor Row	A2
Chester Street	C1	Market Street	B2
Churchbank	B3	Morley Street	C1
Claremont	C1	Neal Street	C1
Croft Street	C2	Nelson Street	C2
Darley Street	A2	North Parade	A2
Drake Street	B2	Otley Road	A3
Drewton Road	A1	Peel Street	B2
Duke Street	A2	Prince's Way	C1
East Parade	B3	Sawrey Place	C2
Eastbrook Lane	B2	Sharpe Street	C2
Forster Square	A3	Shipley Airedale Road	A3
Fountain Street	A1	Simes Street	A1
George Street	B3	Sunbridge Road	B1
Godwin Street	B2	Tetley Street	B1
Grattan Road	B1	Thornton Road	B1
Great Horton Road	C1	Valley Road	A2
Grove Terrace	B1	Vicar Lane	B3
Hall Ings	B2	Wakefield Road	C3
Hamm Strasse	A2	Westgate	A1
Harris Street	B3	White Abbey Road	A1

TOURIST INFORMATION ☎ 01274 753678
NATIONAL MUSEUM OF PHOTOGRAPHY & FILM,
PICTUREVILLE, BRADFORD, W. YORKS, BD1 1NQ

HOSPITAL A & E ☎ 01274 542200
BRADFORD ROYAL INFIRMARY,
DUCKWORTH LANE, BRADFORD, BD9 6RJ

COUNCIL OFFICE ☎ 01274 752111
CITY HALL, CHANNING WAY,
BRADFORD, BD1 1HY

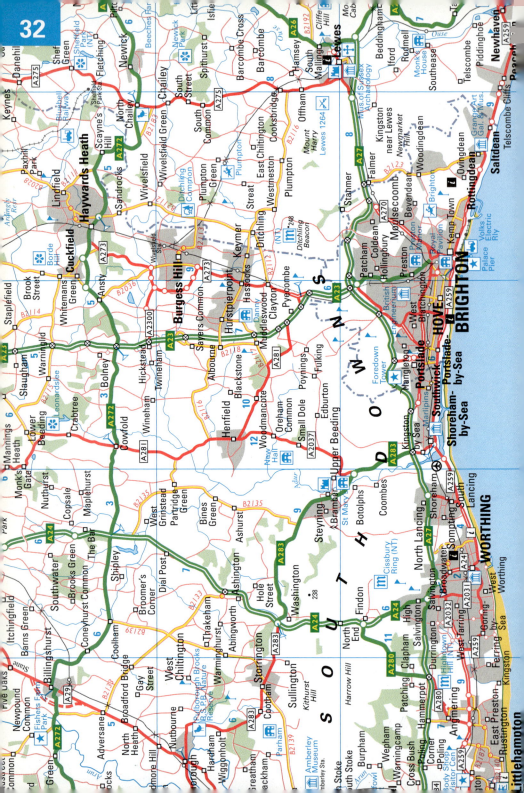

S I D Code 01273

Brighton & Hove

BRIGHTON

Beaconsfield Villas	A2
Bear Road	A3
Bonchurch Road	B3
Buckingham Road	B2
Cheapside	C2
Church Street	C2
Churchill Square	B1
Clifton Hill	A3
Coombe Road	B1
Davey Drive	A3
Davigdor Road	B1
Dewe Road	A3
Ditchling Rise	A2
Dyke Road	A1
Eastern Street	C3
Edward Street	C2
Elm Grove	B3
Florence Road	A2
Freshfield Road	C3
Gloucester Road	B2
Grand Junction Road	C2
Hartington Road	B3
Highcroft Villas	A1
Holland Road	B1
Hollingbury Road	A2
Hollingdean Road	A3
Islingword Road	B3
John Street	C2
King's Road	C1
Lansdowne Road	B1
Lewes Road	B3
London Road	B2
Madeira Drive	C2

Marine Parade	C2
Montefiore Road	B1
Montpelier Road	C1
North Street	C2
Old Shoreham Road	B1
Old Steine	B2
Preston Circus	B2
Preston Drove	A2
Preston Park Avenue	A2
Preston Road	A1
Queen's Park Road	B3
Queen's Road	C2
Richmond Place	B2
Richmond Terrace	C2
St. James's Street	B3
Southover Street	A1
South Road	A2
Stanford Avenue	A1
Stanford Road	A3
The Crestway	B2
The Drove	C2
The Lanes	A1
The Upper Drive	C2
Union Road	B1
Upper Hollingdean Road	B2
Upper Lewes Road	A3
Upper North Street	B2
Viaduct Road	C1
West Street	B1
Western Road	B3
York Avenue	B1
York Place	B2

TOURIST INFORMATION ☎ 01273 292599
10 BARTHOLOMEW SQUARE,
BRIGHTON, BN1 1JS

HOSPITAL A & E ☎ 01273 696955
ROYAL SUSSEX COUNTY HOSPITAL,
EASTERN ROAD, BRIGHTON, BN2 5BE

COUNCIL OFFICE ☎ 01273 290000
TOWN HALL, BARTHOLOMEWS,
BRIGHTON, BN1 1JA

LOCAL RADIO

BBC SOUTHERN COUNTIES RADIO 95.3 FM
SOUTH COAST RADIO 1323 AM, SOUTHERN FM 103.5

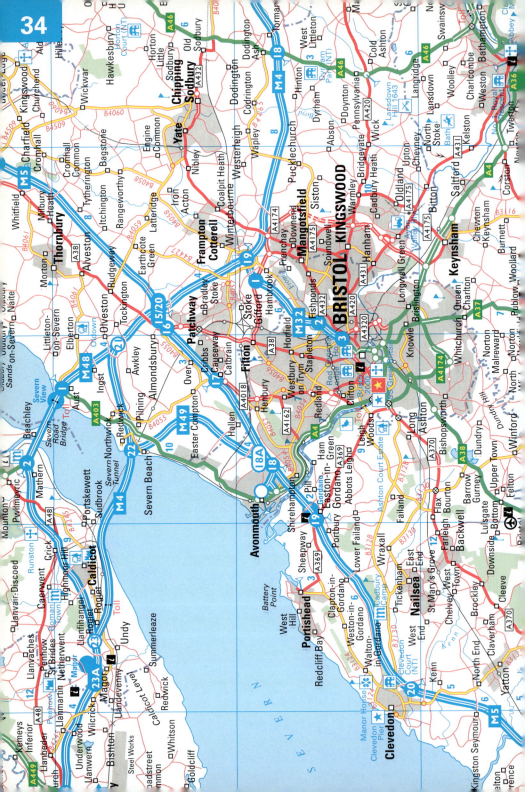

STD Code 0117

BRISTOL

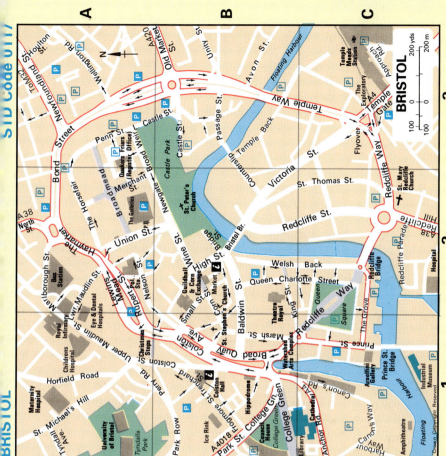

BRISTOL

Crown Copyright Reserved

Anchor Road	C1
Approach Road	C3
Avon Street	B3
Baldwin Street	B1
Bond Street	A2
Bridge Street	B2
Bristol Bridge	B2
Broadmead	A2
Broad Quay	B1
Broad Weir	A3
Canon's Road	C1
Canon's Way	C1
Castle Street	B3
Christmas Steps	A1
College Green	B1
Colston Avenue	B1
Colston Street	B1
Corn Street	B2
Countership	B1
Frogmore Street	B1
Harbour Way	C1
High Street	B2
Horfield Road	A1
Houlton Street	A3
King Street	B2
Lewins Mead	A2
Lower Castle Street	A3
Lower Maudlin Street	A2
Malborough Street	A2
Marsh Street	B1
Merchant Street	A2
Nelson Street	A2
Newfoundland Street	A3
Newgate	B2

North Street	A2
Old Market Street	B3
Park Row	B1
Park Street	B1
Passage Street	B3
Penn Street	A3
Perry Road	B1
Prince Street	C1
Prince Street Bridge	C1
Queen Charlotte Street	B2
Redcliffe Bridge	C2
Redcliffe Hill	C2
Redcliffe Parade	C2
Redcliffe Street	B2
Redcliffe Way	C2
Rupert Street	A1
St. Michael's Hill	C2
St. Thomas Street	B1
Small Street	B3
Temple Back	C3
Temple Gate	C3
Temple Way	C1
The Grove	A2
The Haymarket	A2
The Horsefair	B1
Trenchard Street	A1
Tyndall Avenue	A3
Union Street	A2
Upper Mauldin Street	A2
Victoria Street	B1
Wellington Road	B2
Welsh Back	A3
Wine Street	B2

LOCAL RADIO

BBC RADIO BRISTOL 95.5 FM
BRUNEL CLASSIC GOLD 1260 AM, GWR FM 96.3 FM, GALAXY RADIO 101 FM

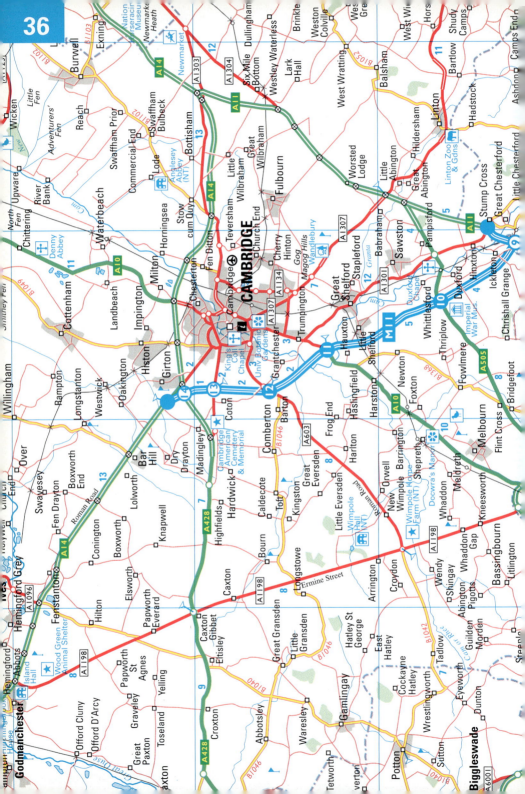

SID Code 01223   Cambridgeshire   CAMBRIDGE

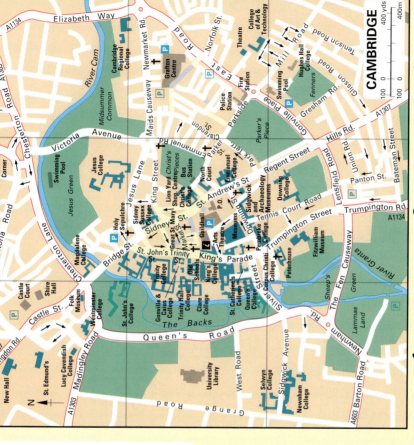

Barton Road	C1
Bateman Street	C2
Bridge Street	A2
Castle Street	A1
Chesterton Lane	A2
Chesterton Road	A2
Clarendon Street	B3
Downing Street	B2
East Road	B3
Elizabeth Way	A3
Emmanuel Road	B2
Fen Causeway, The	C1
Glisson Road	C3
Gonville Place	C3
Grange Road	B1
Gresham Road	C3
Hills Road	C3
Huntingdon Road	A1
Jesus Lane	B2
King's Parade	B2
King Street	B2
Lensfield Road	C2
Madingley Road	A1
Maids Causeway	B3
Market Street	B2

Mill Road	C3
Newmarket Road	B3
Newnham Road	C1
Norfolk Street	B3
Panton Street	C2
Parker Street	B2
Parkside	B3
Park Terrace	B2
Queen's Road	B1
Regent Street	C2
St. Andrew's Street	B2
St. John's Street	B2
Sidgwick Avenue	C1
Sidney Street	B2
Silver Street	C1
Tenison Court Road	C3
Tennis Court Road	B2
Trinity Street	B2
Trumpington Road	C2
Trumpington Street	C2
Union Road	C2
Victoria Avenue	A2
Victoria Road	A2
West Road	B1

LOCAL RADIO

BBC RADIO CAMBRIDGESHIRE 96 FM
Q 103 FM
CAMBRIDGESHIRE 96 FM

TOURIST INFORMATION ☎ 01223 322640
WHEELER STREET, CAMBRIDGE,
CAMBRIDGESHIRE, CB2 3QB

HOSPITAL A & E ☎ 01223 245151
ADDENBROOKE'S HOSPITAL, HILLS ROAD,
CAMBRIDGE, CB2 2QQ

COUNCIL OFFICE ☎ 01223 457000
THE GUILDHALL, MARKET SQUARE,
CAMBRIDGE, CB2 3QJ

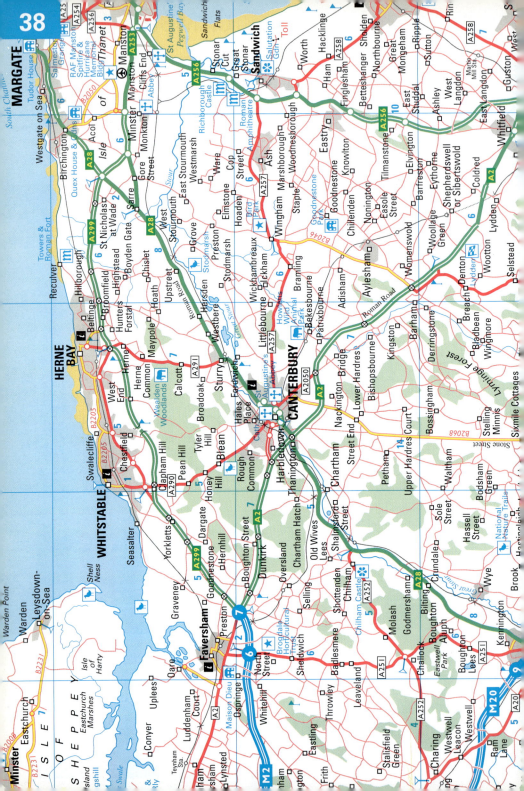

STD Code 01227 · Kent · CANTERBURY

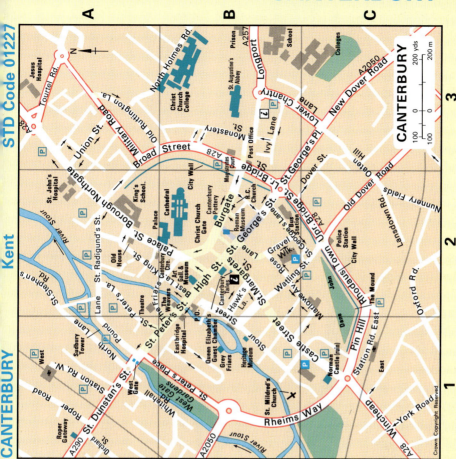

CANTERBURY

200 yds
200 m

Crown Copyright Reserved

LOCAL RADIO
BBC RADIO KENT 97.6 FM
INVICTA RADIO 103.1 FM

TOURIST INFORMATION ☎ 01227 766567
34 ST. MARGARET'S STREET, CANTERBURY,
KENT, CT1 2TG

HOSPITAL A & E ☎ 01227 766877
KENT & CANTERBURY HOSPITAL,
ETHELBERT ROAD, CANTERBURY, CT1 3NG

COUNCIL OFFICE ☎ 01227 763763
COUNCIL OFFICES, MILITARY ROAD,
CANTERBURY, CT1 1YW

STD Code 01222

CARDIFF

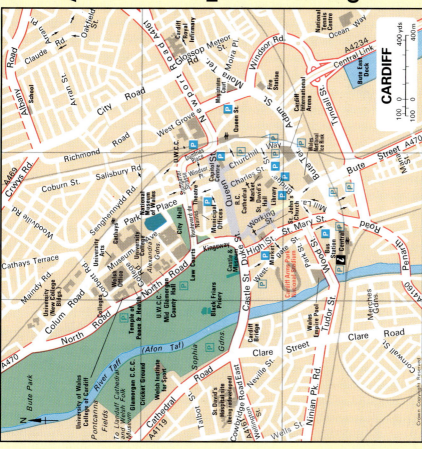

BBC RADIO WALES 882 AM
TOUCH AM 1359 AM, RED DRAGON FM 103.2 FM

LOCAL RADIO

TOURIST INFORMATION ☎ 01222 227281
CENTRAL STATION, CARDIFF, CF1 1QY

HOSPITAL A & E ☎ 01222 492233
CARDIFF ROYAL INFIRMARY, NEWPORT ROAD,
CARDIFF, CF2 1SZ

COUNCIL OFFICE ☎ 01222 872000
COUNTY HALL, ATLANTIC WHARF,
CARDIFF, CF1 5UW

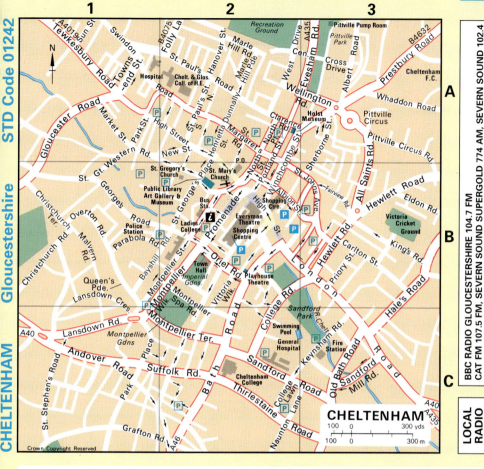

BBC RADIO GLOUCESTERSHIRE 104.7 FM
CAT FM 107.5 FM, SEVERN SOUND SUPERGOLD 774 AM, SEVERN SOUND 102.4

LOCAL RADIO

CHELTENHAM
100   0   300 yds
100   0   300 m

Crown Copyright Reserved

Albert Road	A3	Folly Lane	A2	Marle Hill Road	A2	St. George's Place	B2
Albion Street	B2	Gloucester Road	A1	Montpellier Spa Road	B2	St. George's Road	B1
All Saints Road	B3	Grafton Road	C1	Montpellier Street	B1	St. Margaret's Road	A2
Andover Road	C1	Great Western Road	B1	Montpellier Terrace	C1	St. Paul's Road	A2
Bath Road	C2	Hale's Road	C2	Montpellier Walk	B1	St. Paul's Street North	A2
Bayshill Road	B1	Hanover Street	A2	Naunton Lane	C2	St. Paul's Street South	A2
Carlton Street	B3	Henrietta Street	A2	New Street	A2	St. Stephen's Road	C1
Central Cross Drive	A2	Hewlett Road	B3	North Place	A2	Sandford Mill Road	C3
Christchurch Road	B1	High Street	A2	North Street	B2	Sandford Road	C2
Christchurch Terrace	B1	Keynsham Road	C3	Old Bath Road	C3	Sherborne Street	B3
Clarence Road	A2	King's Road	B3	Oriel Road	B2	Suffolk Road	C1
College Lawn	C2	Lansdown Crescent	B1	Overton Road	B1	Sun Street	A1
College Road	C2	Lansdown Road	C1	Parabola Road	B1	Swindon Road	A1
Dunnally Street	A2	London Road	B3	Park Place	C1	Tewkesbury Road	A1
Eldon Road	B3	Malvern Road	B1	Park Street	A1	Thirlestaine Road	C2
Evesham Road	A3	Market Street	A1	Pittville Circus	A3	Townsend Street	A1
Fairview Road	B3	Marle Hill Parade	A2	Pittville Circus Road	A3	Vittoria Walk	B2
				Portland Street	B2	Wellington Road	A2
				Prestbury Road	A3	West Drive	A2
				Priory Street	B3	Whaddon Road	A3
				Promenade	B2	Winchcombe Street	B2
				Queen's Parade	B1		

TOURIST INFORMATION ☎ 01242 522878
77 THE PROMENADE, CHELTENHAM,
GLOUCESTERSHIRE, GL50 1PP

HOSPITAL A & E ☎ 01242 222222
CHELTENHAM GENERAL HOSPITAL,
SANDFORD ROAD, CHELTENHAM, GL53 7AN

COUNCIL OFFICE ☎ 01242 262626
MUNICIPAL OFFICES, THE PROMENADE,
CHELTENHAM, GL50 1PP

STD Code 01244

Cheshire

CHESTER

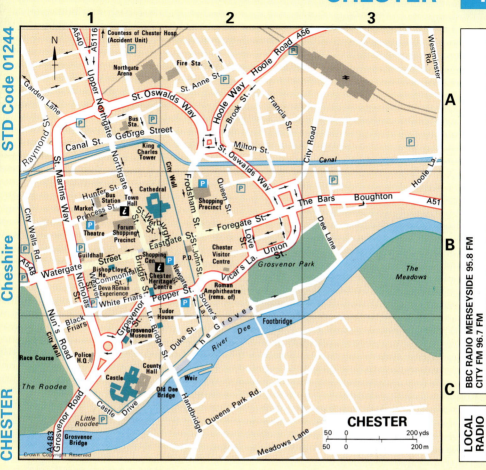

Crown Copyright Reserved

CHESTER

| 50 | 0 | | 200 yds |
| 50 | 0 | | 200 m |

BBC RADIO MERSEYSIDE 95.8 FM
CITY FM 96.7 FM

LOCAL RADIO

Black Friars	C1	Frodsham Street	B2	Milton Street	A2	St. Oswalds Way	A1
Boughton	B3	Garden Lane	A1	Newgate Street	A2	St. Werburgh Street	B1
Bridge Street	B1	George Street	A1	Nicholas Street	B1	Souter's Lane	B2
Brook Street	A2	Grosvenor Bridge	C1	Northgate Street	A1	The Bars	B3
Canal Street	A1	Grosvenor Road	C1	Nun's Road	B1	The Groves	C2
Castle Drive	C1	Grosvenor Street	C1	Old Dee Bridge	C2	Union Street	B2
City Road	A3	Handbridge	C2	Pepper Street	B1	Upper Northgate	A1
City Walls Road	B1	Hoole Lane	B3	Princess Street	B1	Vicar's Lane	B2
Commonhall Street	B1	Hoole Road	A2	Queens Park Road	C2	Watergate Street	B1
Dee Lane	B3	Hoole Way	A2	Queen Street	B2	Weaver Street	B1
Duke Street	C2	Hunter Street	B1	Raymond Street	A1	Westminster Road	A3
Eastgate Street	B1	Love Street	B2	St. Anne Street	A2	White Friars	B1
Foregate Street	B2	Lower Bridge Street	C1	St. John Street	B2		
Francis Street	A2	Meadows Lane	C2	St. Martins Way	A1		

TOURIST INFORMATION ☎ 01244 402111
TOWN HALL, NORTHGATE STREET,
CHESTER, CHESHIRE, CH1 2HJ

HOSPITAL A & E ☎ 01244 365000
COUNTESS OF CHESTER HOSPITAL, HEALTH PK,
LIVERPOOL ROAD, CHESTER, CH2 1UL

COUNCIL OFFICE ☎ 01244 324324
TOWN HALL, MARKET SQUARE,
NORTHGATE STREET, CHESTER, CH1 2HN

STD Code 01203

West Midlands

COVENTRY

BBC RADIO W.M. 94.8/104 FM
CLASSIC GOLD 1359. AM, KIX 96 96.2 FM, MERCIA FM 97 FM

LOCAL RADIO

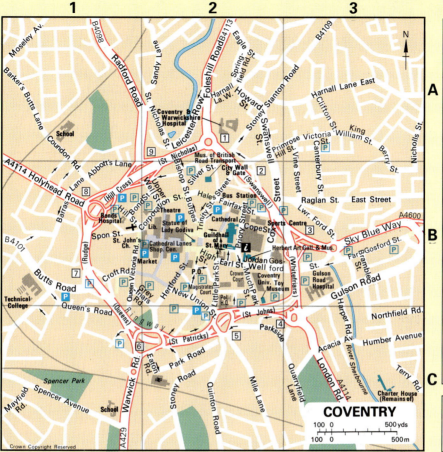

Abbott's Lane	B1	Eagle Street	A2	Hill Street	B1	Radford Road	A1
Acacia Avenue	C3	Earl Street	B2	Holyhead Road	B1	Raglan Street	B3
Barker's Butts Lane	A1	East Street	B3	Howard Street	A2	Ringway	C1
Barras Lane	B1	Eaton Road	C2	Humber Avenue	C3	Rudge (Ringway)	B1
Berry Street	A3	Fairfax Street	B2	Jordan Well	B2	St. Johns (Ringway)	C2
Bishop Street	B2	Far Gosford Street	B3	King William Street	A3	St. Nicholas (Ringway)	A2
Bond Street	B1	Foleshill Road	A2	Leicester Row	A2	St. Nicholas Street	A2
Bramble Street	B3	Gosford Street	B2	Little Park Street	B2	St. Patricks (Ringway)	C2
Burges	B2	Greyfriars Road	B1	London Road	C3	Sandy Lane	A2
Butts Road	B1	Gulson Road	B3	Lower Ford Street	B3	Silver Street	B2
Canterbury Street	A3	Hales Street	B2	Mayfield Road	C1	Sky Blue Way	B3
Clifton Street	A3	Harnall Lane East	A3	Mile Lane	C2	Spencer Avenue	C1
Cope Street	B2	Harnall Lane West	A2	Moseley Avenue	A1	Spon Street	B1
Corporation Street	B2	Harper Road	B3	Much Park Street	B2	Springfield Road	A2
Coundon Road	A1	Hertford Street	B2	New Union Street	B2	Stoney Road	C2
Cox Street	B2	High Street	B2	Nicholls Street	A3	Stoney Stanton Road	A2
Croft Road	B1	Hill Cross (Ringway)	B1	Northfield Road	C3	Swanswell Street	A2
				Park Road	C2	Swanswell (Ringway)	B2
				Parkside	C2	Terry Road	C3
				Primrose Hill Street	A2	Trinity Street	B2
				Priory Street	B2	Upper Well Street	B2
				Quarryfield Lane	C3	Victoria Street	A3
				Queens (Ringway)	C1	Vine Street	A3
				Queen's Road	B1	Warwick Road	C1
				Queen Victoria Road	B1	Whitefriars (Ringway)	B3
				Quinton Road	C2		

TOURIST INFORMATION ☎ 01203 832303/4
BAYLEY LANE, COVENTRY,
WEST MIDLANDS, CV1 5RN

HOSPITAL A & E ☎ 01203 602020
COVENTRY & WARWICKSHIRE HOSPITAL,
STONEY STANTON ROAD, COVENTRY, CV1 4FH

COUNCIL OFFICE ☎ 01203 833333
COUNCIL HOUSE, EARL STREET,
COVENTRY, CV1 5RR

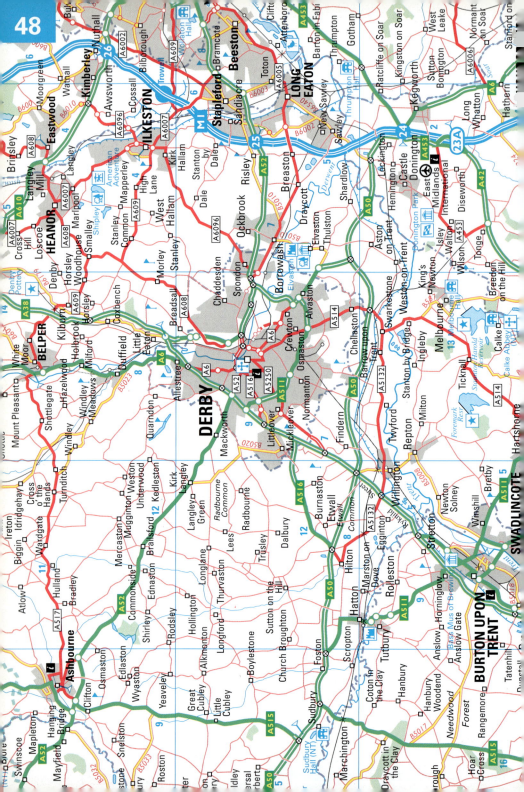

STD Code 01332

DERBY

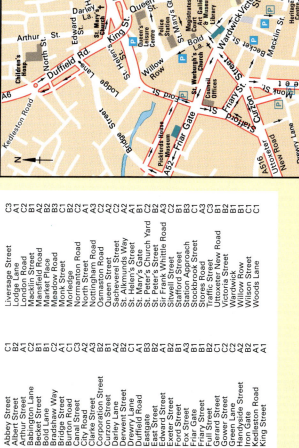

Abbey Street	C1	Liversage Street	C3	
Albert Street	B2	Lodge Lane	A1	
Arthur Street	A1	London Road	C2	
Babington Lane	C2	Macklin Street	B1	
Becket Street	B1	Mansfield Road	A2	
Bold Lane	B1	Market Place	B2	
Bradshaw Way	C2	Meadow Road	B3	
Bridge Street	A1	Monk Street	C1	
Burton Road	C1	Morledge	B2	
Canal Street	C3	Normanton Road	C2	
City Road	A2	North Street	A1	
Clarke Street	A3	Nottingham Road	A3	
Corporation Street	B2	Osmaston Road	C2	
Curzon Street	B1	Queen Street	A2	
Darley Lane	A2	Sacheverel Street	C2	
Derwent Street	B2	St. Alkmunds Way	A2	
Drewry Lane	C1	St. Helen's Way	A1	
Duffield Road	A1	St. Mary's Gate	B1	
Eastgate	B3	St. Peter's Church Yard	C2	
East Street	B2	St. Peter's Street	B2	
Edward Street	A1	Sir Frank Whittle Road	A3	
Exeter Street	B2	Sitwell Street	C2	
Ford Street	B1	Stafford Street	B1	
Fox Street	A3	Station Approach	B3	
Friar Gate	B1	Stockbrook Street	C1	
Friary Street	B1	Stores Road	A3	
Full Street	B2	Traffic Road	B2	
Gerard Street	C1	Uttoxeter New Road	B1	
Gower Street	C2	Victoria Street	B2	
Green Lane	C2	Wardwick	B1	
Handyside Street	A2	Willow Row	A2	
Iron Gate	B2	Wilson Street	C1	
Kedleston Road	A1	Woods Lane	C1	
King Street	A1			

LOCAL RADIO

BBC RADIO DERBY 94.2 FM
RAM FM 102.8 FM

TOURIST INFORMATION ☎ 01332 255802
ASSEMBLY ROOMS, MARKET PLACE,
DERBY, DE1 3AH

HOSPITAL A & E ☎ 01332 347141
DERBYSHIRE ROYAL INFIRMARY,
LONDON ROAD, DERBY, DE1 2QY

COUNCIL OFFICE ☎ 01332 293111
THE COUNCIL HOUSE, CORPORATION STREET,
DERBY, DE1 2FS

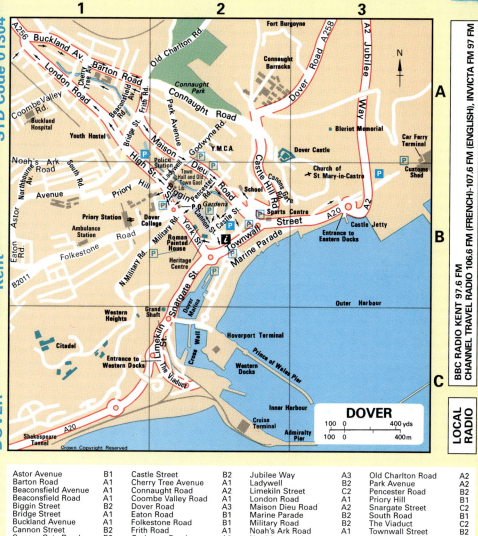

STD Code 01304

Kent

DOVER

BBC RADIO KENT 97.6 FM
CHANNEL TRAVEL RADIO 106.6 FM (FRENCH)-107.6 FM (ENGLISH), INVICTA FM 97 FM

LOCAL RADIO

Astor Avenue	B1	Castle Street	B2	Jubilee Way	A3	Old Charlton Road	A2
Barton Road	A1	Cherry Tree Avenue	A1	Ladywell	B2	Park Avenue	A2
Beaconsfield Avenue	A1	Connaught Road	A2	Limekiln Street	C2	Pencester Road	B2
Beaconsfield Road	A1	Coombe Valley Road	A1	London Road	A1	Priory Hill	B1
Biggin Street	B2	Dover Road	A3	Maison Dieu Road	A2	Snargate Street	C2
Bridge Street	A1	Eaton Road	B1	Marine Parade	B2	South Road	B1
Buckland Avenue	A1	Folkestone Road	B1	Military Road	B2	The Viaduct	C2
Cannon Street	B2	Frith Road	A1	Noah's Ark Road	A1	Townwall Street	B2
Canons Gate Road	B2	Godwyne Road	A2	Northbourne Avenue	B1	York Street	B2
Castle Hill Road	B1	High Street	A1	North Military Road	B1		

TOURIST INFORMATION ☎ 01304 205108
TOWNWALL STREET, DOVER, KENT, CT16 1JR

HOSPITAL A & E ☎ 01304 201624
**BUCKLAND HOSPITAL, COOMBE VALLEY ROAD,
BUCKLAND, DOVER, CT17 OHD**

COUNCIL OFFICE ☎ 01304 821199
**COUNCIL OFFICES, WHITE CLIFFS BUSINESS
PARK, DOVER, CT16 3PG**

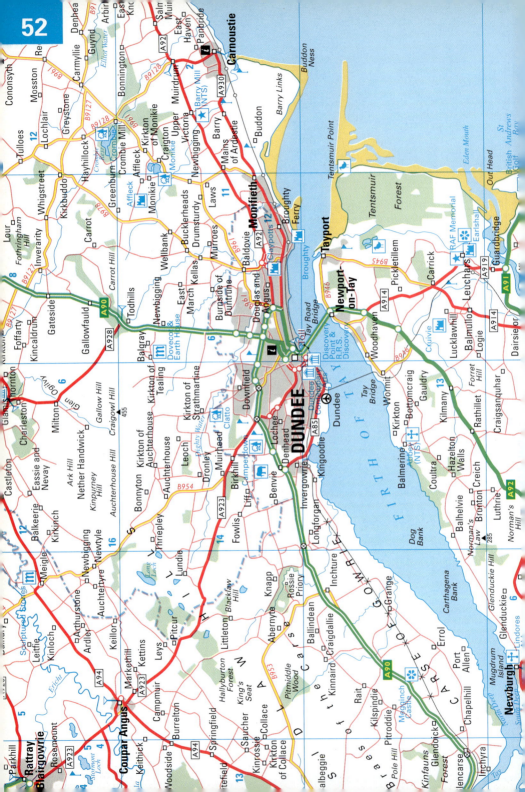

STD Code 01382

DUNDEE

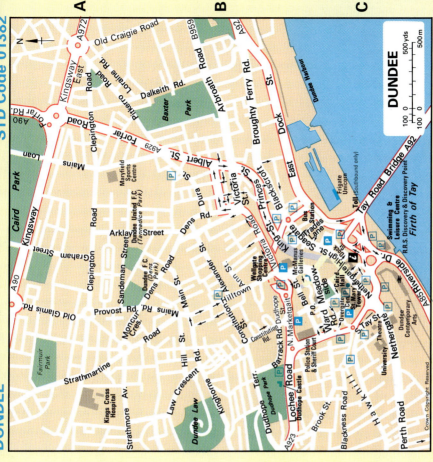

DUNDEE

500yds
500m

Crown Copyright Reserved

LOCAL RADIO

BBC RADIO SCOTLAND 810 AM
RADIO TAY AM 1161 AM, TAY FM 102.8 FM

TOURIST INFORMATION ☎ 01382 434664
4 CITY SQUARE, DUNDEE, DD1 3BA

HOSPITAL A & E ☎ 01382 660111
DUNDEE ROYAL INFIRMARY, BARRACK ROAD,
DUNDEE, DD1 9ND

COUNCIL OFFICE ☎ 01382 434000
CITY CHAMBERS, 21 CITY SQUARE,
DUNDEE, DD1 3BD

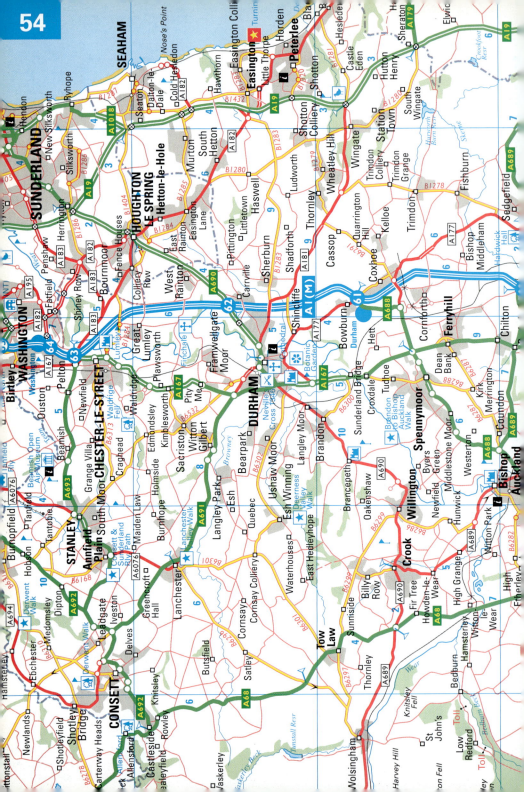

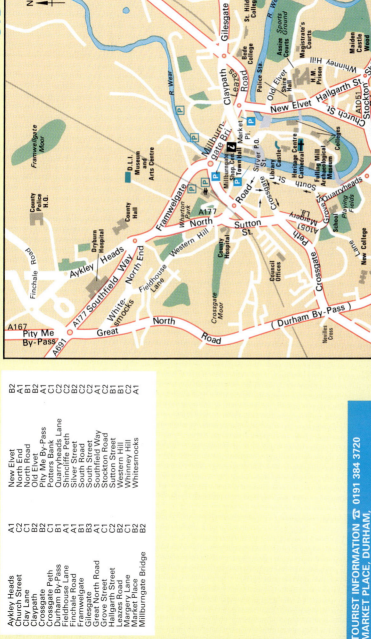

STD Code 0191

DURHAM

TOURIST INFORMATION ☎ 0191 384 3720
MARKET PLACE, DURHAM,
COUNTY DURHAM, DH1 3NJ

HOSPITAL A & E ☎ 0191 333 2333
DRYBURN HOSPITAL, NORTH ROAD,
DURHAM, DH1 5TW

COUNCIL OFFICE ☎ 0191 386 6111
COUNCIL OFFICES, BYLAND LODGE,
HAWTHORN TERRACE, DURHAM, DH1 4TD

STD Code 0131

EDINBURGH

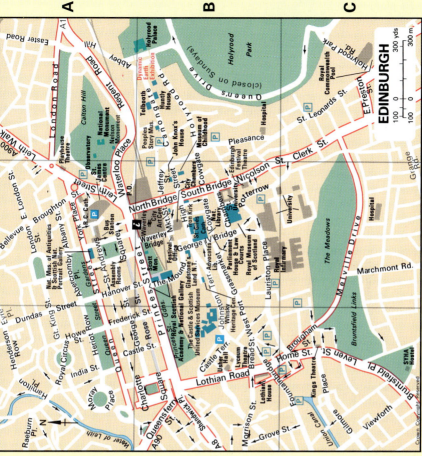

BBC RADIO SCOTLAND 810 AM
MAX AM 1548 AM, FORTH FM 97.3 FM, SCOT FM 101.1 FM

LOCAL RADIO

TOURIST INFORMATION ☎ 0131 557 1700 INFORMATION CENTRE, 3 PRINCES STREET, EDINBURGH, EH2 2QP

HOSPITAL A & E ☎ 0131 536 1000 ROYAL INFIRMARY OF EDINBURGH, 1 LAURISTON PLACE, EDINBURGH, EH3 9YW

COUNCIL OFFICE ☎ 0131 200 2000 CITY CHAMBERS, HIGH STREET, EDINBURGH, EH1 1YJ

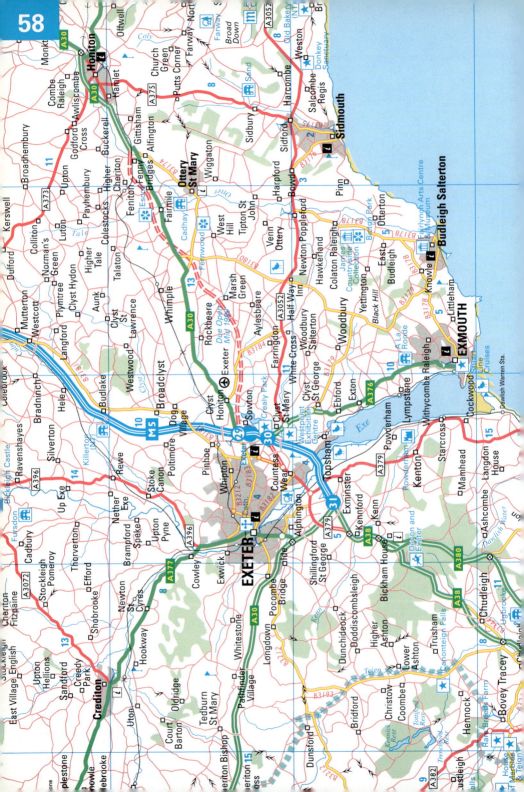

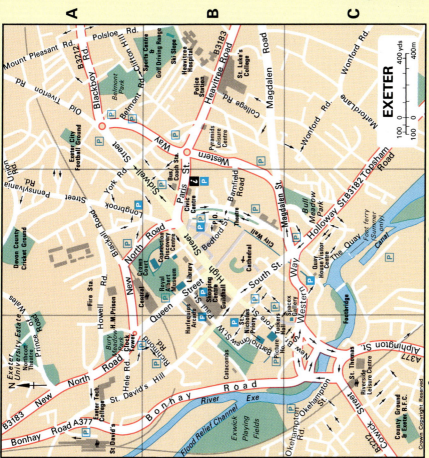

EXETER

LOCAL RADIO

BBC RADIO DEVON 95.8 FM
GEMINI AM 666 AM, GEMINI FM 97 FM

TOURIST INFORMATION ☎ 01392 265700
CIVIC CENTRE, PARIS STREET, EXETER
DEVON, EX1 1RP

HOSPITAL A & E ☎ 01392 411611
ROYAL DEVON & EXETER HOSPITAL (WONFORD),
BARRACK ROAD, EXETER, EX2 5DW

COUNCIL OFFICE ☎ 01392 277888
CIVIC CENTRE, PARIS STREET,
EXETER, EX1 1JN

DEAL

Deal
Walmer Castle & Garden
Walmer
Kingsdown
Ringwould
Kingswould

St Margaret's Bay
St Margaret's at Cliffe
The Pines
South Foreland

Worth
Hacklinge
Ham
Finglesham
Eastry
A258 6
Betteshanger
Sholden
Northbourne
Ripple
Sutton
Great Mongeham
A258

St Margaret's Bay
West Cliffe
Guston

A256 10
East Studdal
Ashley
Woollage Green
Nonington

Tilmanstone
Elvington
Eythorne
Shepherdswell or Sibertswold
Coldred
East Langdon
West Langdon
Martin Mill Sta.

Whitfield
A2
Buckland
Maxton
Farthingloe

DOVER

Calais ½ hr – 1½ hrs, Oostende 2hrs
Channel Tunnel

White Cliffs Experience
Knights Templar Church

Staple
Goodnestone Park
Goodnestone
Chillenden
Easole Street
Barfreston
Shepherdswell
A2 6
Lydden
Ewell Minnis
Alkham
Drellingore
West Hougham

St-Radigund's Abbey
East Wear Bay

FOLKESTONE

Boulogne 1hr

B2046
Womenswold
Aylesham
Roman Road
Wootton
Denton
Lydden
Selstead
A260
Swingfield Minnis
Densole
Capel le Ferne
Hawkinge
A20
Rotunda Amusement Park
Sandgate

Bramling
Bekesbourne
Patrixbourne
Adisham
Barham
Derringstone
Breach
Bladbean
Wingmore
Elham
Acrise Place
Paddlesworth
Newington
Etchinghill
13
Cheriton
Channel Tunnel Terminal
B2065

Hythe

Kingston
Bishopsbourne
Lower Hardres
Nackington Bridge
A2050 A2
7
Bossingham
Stelling Minnis
Ottinge
Lyminge
Rhodes Minnis
Sixmile Cottages
Newbarn
Beachborough
12
11A
4
Romney, Hythe & Dymchurch Rly

Chartham Hatch
Old Wives Lees
Shalmsford Street
Pether
Upper Hardres Court
Waltham
Stelling Minnis
Stone Street
B2068
Bodsham Green
Lyminge
Stowting
Postling
Stanford
11
A20
West Hythe
Lympne
A261
2
Saltwood
5
Westenhanger Sta.
A259

Selling
Chilham Castle
Chilham
A252
5
Molash
Godmersham
A28
Crundale
Wye
Brook
Hastingleigh
Lymbridge Green
Brabourne
Brabourne Lees
Smeeth
Sellindge
Stonestreet Green
Aldington
Court-at-Street
Lympne Port
B2067
A20
M20

ASHFORD

Chartham
Street End
Sole Street
Hassell Street
National Trust Trails
Willesborough Lees
Hinxhill
Sevington
Mersham
Kingsnorth
Cheeseman's Green
Swanton Green Mill
Stone Cross
Bilsington
A2070
Ruckinge
Hamstreet
A2070

Sheldwich
Badlesmere
Leaveland
Eastwell Park
Boughton Lees
Kennington
Willesborough
Bonnington
R o m n e y   M a r s h
Newchurch
Snave
St Mary in the Marsh

Selling
Shottenden
Chiham
Biltng
Boughton Aluph
Challock
Boughton Lees
A251
A2042
A2228
Burmarsh
Dymchurch
Martello Tower

A251
9
A20
Kingsnorth
Bilsington
The Dragon Snargate
A2070

STD Code 01303

Kent

FOLKESTONE

FOLKESTONE

200 yds
200 m

Alder Road	B2	High Street	C3
Bathurst Road	C1	Hill Road	A3
Black Bull Road	B2	Joyes Road	A3
Bournemouth Road	B2	Links Way	A1
Bouverie Road West	C1	Lower Sandgate Road	C2
Bradstone Road	B2	Lucy Avenue	A1
Broadmead Road	B2	Manor Road	C2
Canterbury Road	A2/B3	Marine Parade	C2
Castle Hill Avenue	C2	Park Farm Road	A2
Cheriton Gardens	C2	Pavilion Road	B2
Cheriton Road	B2	Radnor Bridge Road	B3
Cherry Garden Avenue	B1	Radnor Park Avenue	B2
Churchill Avenue	A1	Radnor Park Road	B1
Coniston Road	B1	Radnor Park West	B1
Coolinge Road	B2	Sandgate Hill	C1
Cornwallis Avenue	B1	Sandgate Road	C2
Dolphins Road	A2	Shorncliffe Road	B1
Dover Road	B2	Sidney Street	B1
Downs Road	A2	The Leas	C2
Earles Avenue	C1	The Stade	B3
Foord Road	B2	The Tram Raod	B3
Foreland Avenue	A3	Tontine Street	B3
Grimston Avenue	C1	Turketel Road	C1
Guildhall Street	C2	Wear Bay Crescent	A3
Guildhall Street North	B2	Wear Bay Road	A3
Harbour Way	B3	Wilton Road	B1

LOCAL RADIO

BBC RADIO KENT 97.6 FM
CHANNEL TRAVEL RADIO 106.6 FM (FRENCH)-107.6 FM (ENGLISH), INVICTA FM 97 FM

TOURIST INFORMATION ☎ 01303 258594
HARBOUR STREET, FOLKESTONE,
KENT, CT20 1QN

HOSPITAL A & E ☎ 01233 633331
WILLIAM HARVEY HOSPITAL, KENNINGTON RD,
WILLESBOROUGH, ASHFORD, TN24 OLZ

COUNCIL OFFICE ☎ 01303 850388
CIVIC CENTRE, CASTLE HILL AVENUE,
FOLKESTONE, CT20 2QY

© Crown Copyright Reserved

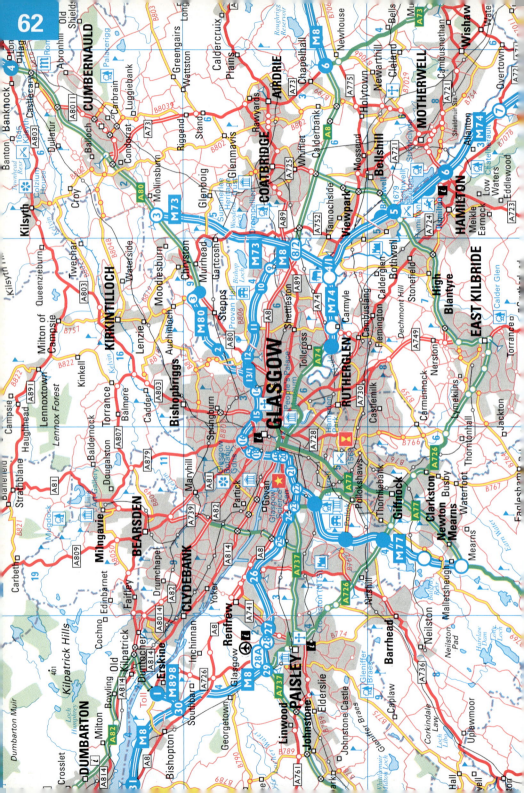

GLASGOW

63

STD Code 0141

GLASGOW

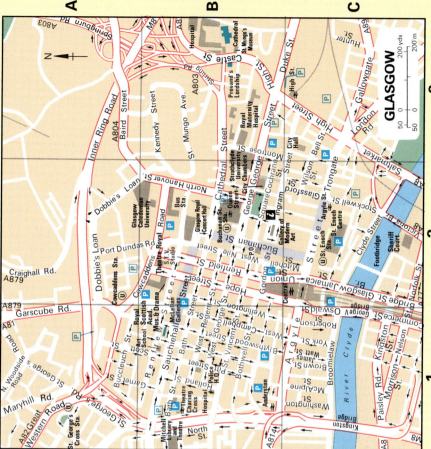

Argyle Street	C1		Kingston Street	C1
Baird Street	A3		London Road	C3
Bath Street	B1		Maryhill Road	A1
Bell Street	C3		McAlpine Street	C1
Blythswood Street	B1		Mitchell Street	C2
Bothwell Street	B1		Montrose Street	B3
Bridge Street	C2		Morrison Street	C1
Broomielaw	C1		Nelson Street	C1
Brown Street	C1		Norfolk Street	C2
Buccleuch Street	A1		North Hanover Street	B2
Buchanan Street	B2		North Street	B1
Castle Street	B3		North Woodside Road	A1
Cathedral Street	B2		Oswald Street	C1
Clyde Street	C2		Paisley Road	C1
Cochrane Street	B2		Pitt Street	B1
Commerce Street	C1		Port Dundas Road	A2
Cowcaddens Road	A2		Queen Street	B2
Craighall Road	A1		Renfield Street	B2
Dobbie's Loan	A2		Renfrew Street	B1
Duke Street	B3		Robertson Street	C1
Gallowgate	C3		Saltmarket	C2
Garnet Street	A1		Sauchiehall Street	B1
Garscube Road	A1		Scott Street	A1
George Square	B2		Springburn Road	A3
George Street	B2		St. George's Road	A1
George V Bridge	C1		St. Mungo Avenue	B3
Glasgow Bridge	C2		St. Vincent Street	B1
Glassford Street	C2		Stirling Road	B3
Gordon Street	B2		Stockwell Street	C2
Great Western Road	A1		Trongate	C2
High Street	B3		Union Street	C2
Holland Street	B1		Victoria Bridge	C2
Hope Street	B1		Washington Street	C1
Hunter Street	C3		Wellington Street	B1
Ingram Street	B2		West Campbell Street	B1
Inner Ring Road	A3		West George Street	B1
Jamaica Street	C2		West Nile Street	B2
James Watt Street	C1		West Regent Street	B1
Kennedy Street	B3		Wilson Street	C2
Kingston Bridge	C1		York Street	C1

LOCAL RADIO

BBC RADIO SCOTLAND 810 AM
CLYDE 2 1152 AM, CLYDE 1 102.5 FM, SCOT FM 103 FM

TOURIST INFORMATION ☎ 0141 204 4400
11 GEORGE SQUARE, GLASGOW, G2 1DY

HOSPITAL A & E ☎ 0141 211 2000
WESTERN INFIRMARY, DUMBARTON ROAD,
GLASGOW, G11 6NT

COUNCIL OFFICE ☎ 0141 287 2000
CITY CHAMBERS, GEORGE SQUARE,
GLASGOW, G2 1DU

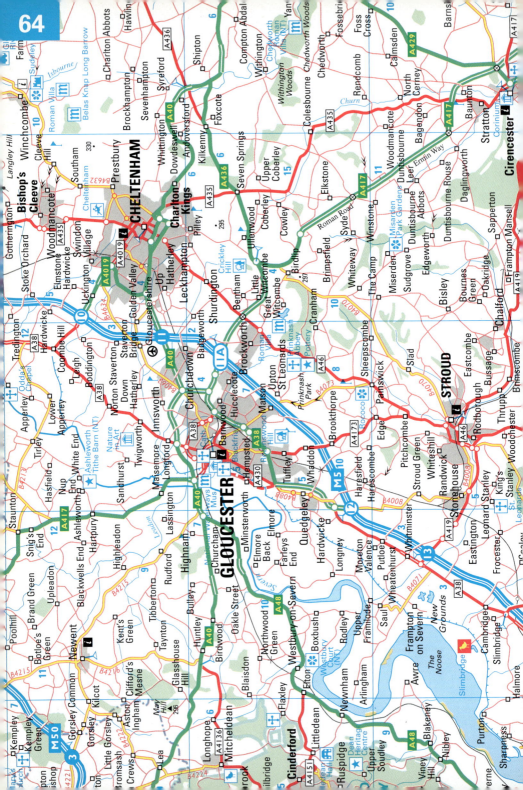

GLOUCESTER · Gloucestershire · STD Code 01452

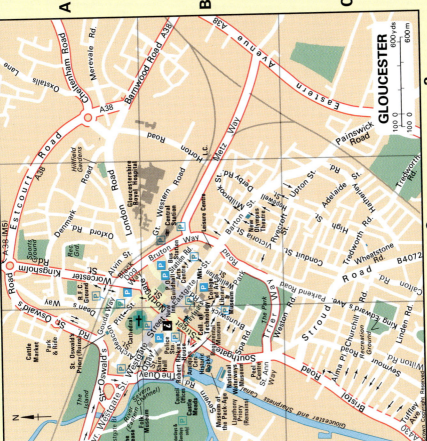

N

GLOUCESTER

600 yds
600 m

Street	Grid	Street	Grid
Adelaide Street	C2	Metz Way	B3
Alma Place	C1	Millbrook Street	B2
Alvin Street	A2	Northgate Street	B1
Archdeacon Street	A1	Oxford Road	A2
Barnwood Road	A3	Oxstalls Lane	A3
Barton Street	B2	Painswick Road	C3
Black Dog Way	A2	Park Road	B2
Bristol Road	C1	Parkend Road	C2
Brunswick Road	B1	Pitt Street	A1
Bruton Way	B2	Quay Street	B1
Calton Road	C2	Ryecroft Street	B2
Cheltenham Road	A3	St. Ann Way	B1
Churchill Road	C1	St. Oswald's Road	A1
Conduit Street	C1	Severn Road	B1
Dean's Way	A1	Seymour Road	C1
Denmark Road	A2	Southgate Street	B1
Derby Road	B2	Spa Road	B1
Estcourt Road	A2	Station Road	B2
Eastern Avenue	C3	Stroud Road	C1
Eastgate Street	B2	The Docks	B1
Gouda Way	A1	The Quay	B1
Great Western Road	B2	Tredworth Road	C2
Greyfriars	B1	Trier Way	B1
Hatherley Road	C2	Tuffley Avenue	C1
High Street	C2	Upton Street	C2
Hopewell Street	C2	Victoria Street	C2
Horton Road	B3	Wellington Street	B2
King Edward's Avenue	C1	Weston Road	A1
Kingsholm Road	A2	Westgate Street	B1
Linden Road	C1	Wheatstone Road	C1
London Road	A2	Wilton Road	C2
Lower Westgate Street	A1	Worcester Street	A2
Merevale Road	A3		

TOURIST INFORMATION ☎ 01452 421188
28 SOUTHGATE STREET, GLOUCESTER,
GLOUCESTERSHIRE, GL1 2BP

HOSPITAL A & E ☎ 01452 528555
GLOUCESTER ROYAL HOSPITAL
GREAT WESTERN RD, GLOUCESTER, GL1 3NN

COUNCIL OFFICE ☎ 01452 522232
COUNCIL OFFICES, NORTH WAREHOUSE,
THE DOCKS, GLOUCESTER, GL1 2EP

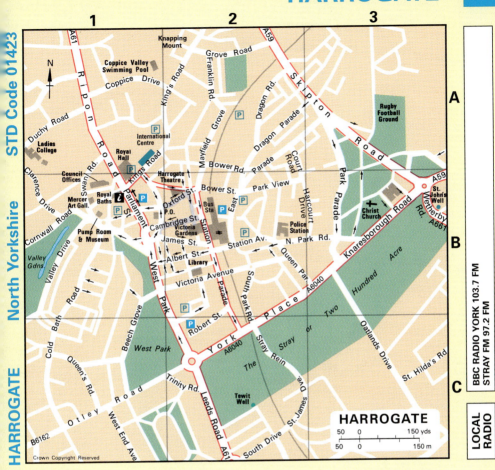

HARROGATE

Scale:
50 — 0 — 150 yds
50 — 0 — 150 m

Crown Copyright Reserved

STD Code 01423

North Yorkshire

HARROGATE

Street	Grid	Street	Grid	Street	Grid	Street	Grid
Albert Street	B2	East Parade	B2	Park Parade	B3	Station Parade	B2
Beech Grove	C1	Franklin Road	A2	Park View	B2	Stray Rein	C2
Bower Road	A2	Grove Road	A2	Parliament Street	B1	Swan Road	B1
Bower Street	B2	Harcourt Drive	B3	Queen Parade	B2	Trinity Road	C2
Cambridge Street	B1	James Street	B2	Queen's Road	C1	Valley Drive	B1
Clarence Drive	B1	King's Road	B1	Ripon Road	A1	Victoria Avenue	B2
Cold Bath Road	C1	Knaresborough Road	B3	Robert Street	C2	West End Avenue	C1
Coppice Drive	A1	Leeds Road	C2	St. Hilda's Road	C3	West Park	B1
Cornwall Road	B1	Mayfield Grove	A2	St. James Drive	C2	Wetherby Road	B3
Court Road	A2	North Park Road	B2	Skipton Road	A2	York Place	C2
Dragon Parade	A2	Oatlands Drive	C3	South Drive	C2		
Dragon Road	A2	Otley Road	C1	South Park Road	B2		
Duchy Road	A1	Oxford Street	B2	Station Avenue	B2		

TOURIST INFORMATION ☎ 01423 537300
ROYAL BATHS ASSEMBLY ROOMS, CRES. ROAD,
HARROGATE, NORTH YORKSHIRE, HG1 2RR

HOSPITAL A & E ☎ 01423 885959
HARROGATE DISTRICT HOSPITAL,
LANCASTER PARK ROAD, HARROGATE, HG2 7SX

COUNCIL OFFICE ☎ 01423 568954
COUNCIL OFFICES, CRESCENT GARDENS
HARROGATE, HG1 2SG

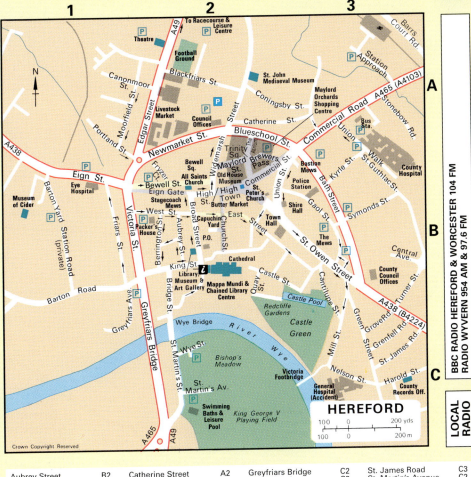

HEREFORD

STD Code 01432

Herefordshire

HEREFORD

BBC RADIO HEREFORD & WORCESTER 104 FM
RADIO WYVERN 954 AM & 97.6 FM

LOCAL RADIO

Aubrey Street	B2	Catherine Street	A2	Greyfriars Bridge	C2	St. James Road	C3
Barrs Court Road	A3	Central Avenue	B3	Grove Road	C3	St. Martin's Avenue	C2
Barton Road	B1	Church Street	B2	Harold Street	C3	St. Martin's Street	C2
Barton Yard	B1	Commercial Road	A3	High Street	B2	St. Owen Street	B3
Bath Street	B3	Commercial Street	B2	High Town	B2	Station Approach	A3
Berrington Street	B2	Coningsby Street	A2	King Street	B2	Station Road	B1
Bewell Street	B2	East Street	B2	Kyrle Street	B3	Stonebow Road	A3
Blackfriars Street	A2	Edgar Street	A2	Maylord Street	B2	Symonds Street	B3
Blueschool Street	A2	Eign Gate	B2	Mill Street	C3	Turner Street	B3
Bridge Street	B2	Eign Street	B1	Moorfield Street	A1	Union Street	B2
Broad Street	B2	Friars Street	B1	Nelson Street	C3	Union Walk	A3
Canonmoor Street	A1	Gaol Street	B3	Newmarket Street	A2	Victoria Street	B1
Cantilupe Street	B3	Green Street	C3	Portland Street	A1	West Street	B2
Capuchin Court	B2	Grenfell Road	C3	Quay Street	B2	Widemarsh Street	A2
Castle Street	B2	Greyfriars Avenue	C1	St. Guthiac Street	B3	Wye Street	C2

TOURIST INFORMATION ☎ **01432 268430**
1 KING STREET, HEREFORD, HR4 9BW

HOSPITAL A & E ☎ **01432 355444**
HEREFORD GENERAL HOSPITAL,
NELSON STREET, HEREFORD, HR1 2PA

COUNCIL OFFICE ☎ **01432 364500**
COUNCIL OFFICES, ST. OWEN STREET,
HEREFORD, HR1 2PJ

STD Code 01463

Highland

INVERNESS

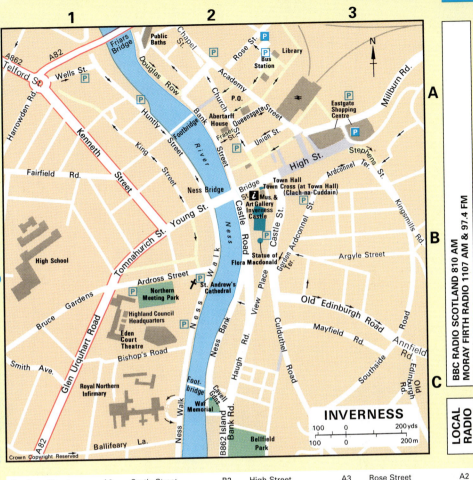

BBC RADIO SCOTLAND 810 AM
MORAY FIRTH RADIO 1107 AM & 97.4 FM

LOCAL RADIO

INVERNESS

100   0   200yds
100   0   200m

TOURIST INFORMATION ☎ 01463 234353
CASTLE WYND, INVERNESS, HIGHLAND, IV2 3BJ

HOSPITAL A & E ☎ 01463 704000
RAIGMORE HOSPITAL, OLD PERTH ROAD,
INVERNESS, IV2 3UJ

COUNCIL OFFICE ☎ 01463 702000
COUNCIL OFFICES, GLENURQUHART ROAD,
INVERNESS, IV3 5NX

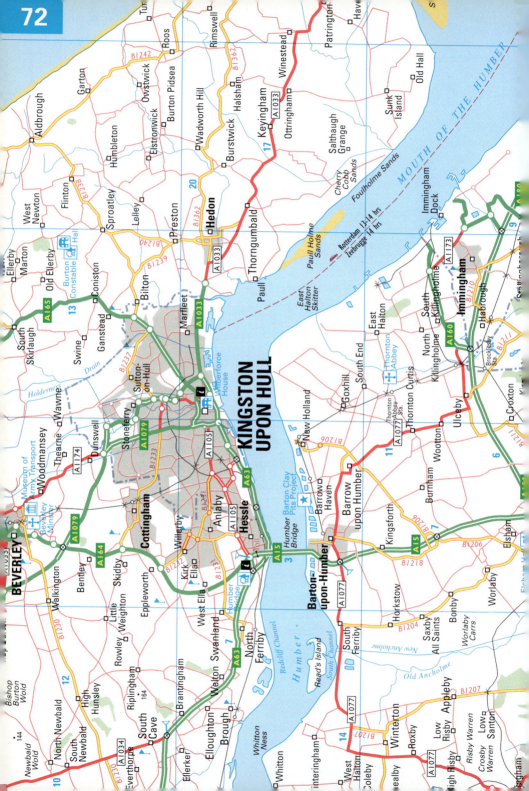

STD Code 01482

KINGSTON UPON HULL

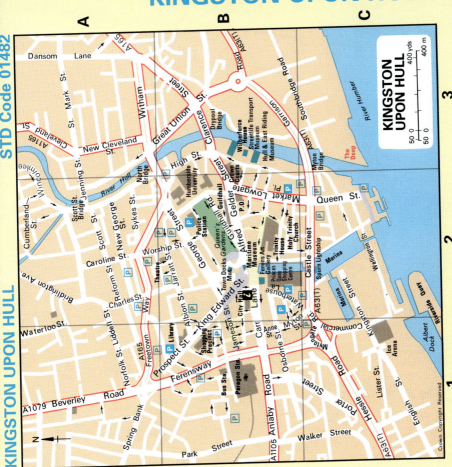

KINGSTON UPON HULL

Crown Copyright Reserved

Albion Street	B1	Liddell Street	A1
Alfred Gelder Street	B2	Lister Street	C1
Anlaby Road	B1	Lowgate	B2
Anne Street	A1	Market Place	B2
Beverley Road	A2	Myton Street	B1
Bridlington Avenue	A2	Mytongate	C1
Caroline Street	B1	New Cleveland Street	A3
Carr Lane	C2	New George Street	A2
Castle Street	A2	Norfolk Street	A1
Charles Street	B3	North Bridge	B1
Clarence Street	A3	Osborne Street	A2
Cleveland Street	C1	Park Street	B1
Commercial Road	A2	Porter Street	A1
Cumberland Street	A3	Prospect Street	C2
Dansom Lane	C1	Queen Street	A2
English Street	B1	Reform Street	A3
Ferensway	A1	St. Mark Street	A2
Freetown Way	B3	Scott Street	A2
Garrison Road	B2	Scott Street Bridge	C3
George Street	B3	Southbridge Road	A1
Great Union Street	B2	Spring Bank	A2
Guildhall Road	C1	Sykes Street	B1
Hessle Road	B3	Walker Street	B2
High Street	B1	Waterhouse Lane	A1
Jameson Street	B2	Waterloo Street	A2
Jarratt Street	A2	Wellington Street	C2
Jenning Street	B1	Wincolmlee	A3
King Edward Street	C1	Witham	A3
Kingston Street		Worship Street	A2

LOCAL RADIO

BBC RADIO HUMBERSIDE 95.9 FM
VIKING FM 96.9 FM, GREAT YORKSHIRE GOLD 1161 AM

TOURIST INFORMATION ☎ 01482 223344
CITY INFORMATION SERVICE, CEN. LIBRARY,
ALBION ST, KINGSTON UPON HULL, HU1 3TF

HOSPITAL A & E ☎ 01482 328541
HULL ROYAL INFIRMARY, ANLABY ROAD,
KINGSTON UPON HULL, HU3 2JZ

COUNCIL OFFICE ☎ 01482 610610
GUILDHALL, ALFRED GELDER STREET,
KINGSTON UPON HULL, HU1 2AA

STD Code 0113

West Yorkshire

LEEDS

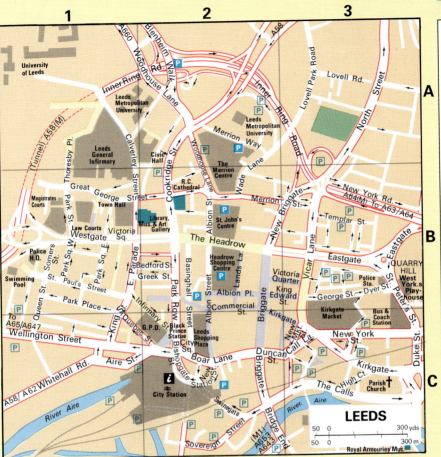

BBC RADIO LEEDS 92.4 FM
MAGIC 828 AM, 96.3 AIRE FM

LOCAL RADIO

Aire Street	C1	Duncan Street	C2	Merrion Street	B2	Sovereign Street	C2
Albion Place	B2	Dyer Street	B3	Merrion Way	A2	St. Paul's Street	B1
Albion Street	B2	East Parade	B1	New Briggate	B2	St. Peter's Street	B3
Basinghall Street	B2	Eastgate	B3	New Market Street	C3	Swinegate	C2
Bedford Street	B1	George Street	B3	New Station Street	C2	Templar Street	B3
Bishopgate Street	C2	Great George Street	B1	New York Road	B3	The Calls	C3
Blenheim Walk	A2	Greek Street	B1	New York Street	C3	The Headrow	B2
Boar Lane	C2	High Court	C3	North Street	A3	Thoresby Place	B1
Bridge End	C2	Infirmary Street	B1	Park Place	B1	Vicar Lane	B3
Briggate	C2	Inner Ring Road	A1	Park Row	B2	Victoria Quarter	B2
Call Lane	C3	King Edward Street	B2	Park Square East	B1	Victoria Square	B1
Calverley Street	A1	King Street	C1	Park Square West	B1	Wade Lane	B2
City Square	C2	Kirkgate	C3	Park Street	B1	Wellington Street	C1
Commercial Street	B2	Lands Lane	B2	Quebec Street	C1	Westgate	B1
Cookridge Street	B2	Lovell Park Road	A3	Queen Street	B1	Whitehall Road	C1
Duke Street	C3	Lovell Road	A3	Somers Street	B1	Woodhouse Lane	A1

TOURIST INFORMATION ☎ 0113 242 5242
REGIONAL TRAVEL CENTRE, THE ARCADE,
CITY STATION, LEEDS, W. YORKSHIRE, LS1 1PL

HOSPITAL A & E ☎ 0113 243 2799
LEEDS GENERAL INFIRMARY,
GREAT GEORGE STREET, LEEDS, LS1 3EX

COUNCIL OFFICE ☎ 0113 234 8080
CIVIC HALL, CALVERLEY STREET,
LEEDS, LS1 1UR

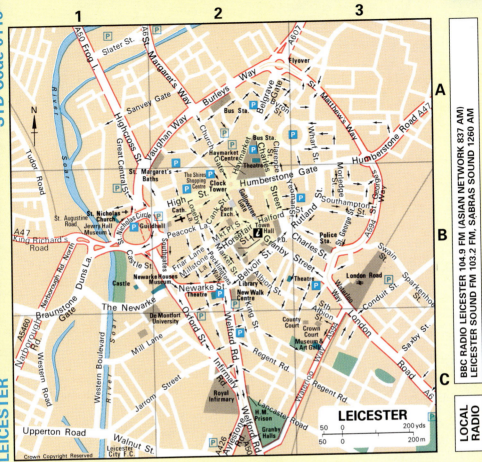

LEICESTER

STD Code 0116

BBC RADIO LEICESTER 104.9 FM (ASIAN NETWORK 837 AM)
LEICESTER SOUND FM 103.2 FM, SABRAS SOUND 1260 AM

LOCAL RADIO

TOURIST INFORMATION ☎ 0116 265 0555
7 - 9 EVERY STREET, TOWN HALL SQUARE,
LEICESTER, LE1 6AG

HOSPITAL A & E ☎ 0116 254 1414
LEICESTER ROYAL INFIRMARY,
INFIRMARY SQUARE, LEICESTER, LE1 5WW

COUNCIL OFFICE ☎ 0116 254 9922
COUNCIL OFFICES, NEW WALK CENTRE,
WELFORD PLACE, LEICESTER, LE1 6ZG

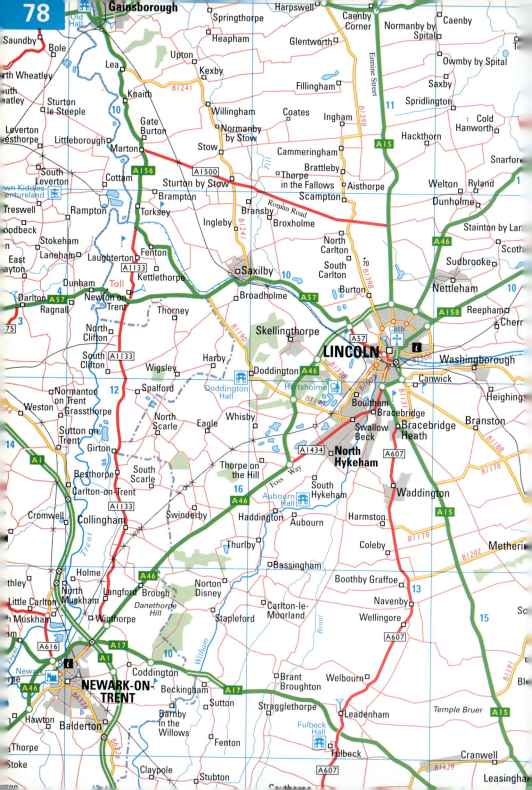

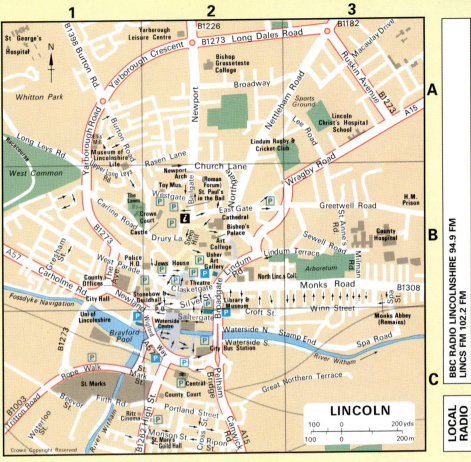

STD Code 01522

Lincolnshire

LINCOLN

BBC RADIO LINCOLNSHIRE 94.9 FM
LINCS FM 102.2 FM

LOCAL RADIO

Bailgate	B2	Great Northern Terrace	C2	Newport	A2	Stamp End	C2
Beevor Street	C1	Greetwell Road	B3	Northgate	B2	Steep Hill	B2
Broadgate	C2	Gresham Street	B1	Pelham Bridge	C2	The Avenue	B1
Broadway	A2	High Street	C2	Portland Street	C2	Tritton Road	C1
Burton Road	A1	Lee Road	A3	Rasen Lane	A2	Upper Long Leys Road	B1
Canwick Road	C2	Lindum Road	B2	Ripon Street	C2	Waterloo Street	C1
Carholme Road	B1	Lindum Terrace	B2	Rope Walk	C1	Waterside North	C2
Carline Road	B1	Long Dales Road	A2	Ruskin Avenue	A3	Waterside South	C2
Church Lane	B2	Long Leys Road	A1	St. Anne's Road	B3	West Parade	B1
Clasketgate	B2	Macaulay Drive	A3	St. Mark Street	C1	Westgate	B2
Croft Street	C2	Milman Road	B3	Saltergate	C2	Wigford Way	C2
Cross Street	C2	Monks Road	B3	Sewell Road	B3	Winn Street	C3
Drury Lane	B2	Monson Street	C2	Silver Street	B2	Wragby Road	B3
East Gate	B2	Nettleham Road	A2	Spa Road	C3	Yarborough Crescent	A1
Firth Road	C1	Newland	B1	Spa Street	B3	Yarborough Road	B1

TOURIST INFORMATION ☎ 01522 529828
9 CASTLE HILL, LINCOLN,
LINCOLNSHIRE, LN1 3AA

HOSPITAL A & E ☎ 01522 512512
LINCOLN COUNTY HOSPITAL,
GREETWELL ROAD, LINCOLN, LN2 5QY

COUNCIL OFFICE ☎ 01522 511511
CITY HALL, BEAUMONT FEE,
LINCOLN, LN1 1DD

LIVERPOOL

Argyle Street	C2	Moorfields	B2
Bath Street	A1	Mount Pleasant	B3
Bold Street	C3	New Quay	B1
Brunswick Street	B1	North John Street	B2
Byrom Street	A3	Old Hall Street	A1
Canning Place	C2	Pall Mall	A1
Castle Street	B2	Paradise Street	C2
Chapel Street	B1	Park Lane	C2
Cheapside	A2	Parker Street	B3
Christian Street	A3	Preston Street	B2
Church Street	B2	Ranelagh Street	B3
Concert Street	C3	Renshaw Street	B3
Cook Street	B2	Roe Street	B3
Copperas Hill	B3	Salthouse Quay	C1
Crosshall Street	B2	School Lane	A3
Dale Street	B2	Scotland Road	A3
Derby Square	C2	Seel Street	B2
Duke Street	B3	Sir Thomas Street	C3
Elliot Street	A2	Skelhorne Street	A3
Gt. Crosshall Street	A1	Slater Street	C1
Gt. Howard Street	C2	South John Street	B3
Hanover Street	C1	St. Anne Street	B1
Hartley Quay	B3	St. John's Lane	C1
Hatton Garden	A2	St. Nicholas Place	A2
Hawke Street	B3	Strand Street	B2
James Street	A1	The Strand	B1
King Edward Street	A1	Tithebarn Street	A3
Kingsway	B3	Vauxhall Road	B3
Leeds Street	A3	Victoria Street	A1
Lime Street	B2	Wapping	A2
London Road	B2	Water Street	B1
Lord Street	B2	Waterloo Road	B2
Manchester Street	C2	Whitechapel	A3
Marybone	A2	William Brown Street	

LOCAL RADIO

BBC RADIO MERSEYSIDE 95.8 FM
RADIO CITY GOLD 1548 AM, CITY FM 96.7 FM

TOURIST INFORMATION ☎ 0151 709 3631
MERSEYSIDE WELCOME CENTRE, CLAYTON SQ.
SHOPPING CEN, LIVERPOOL, MERSEYSIDE, L1 1QR

HOSPITAL A & E ☎ 0151 525 5980
FAZAKERLEY HOSPITAL, LOWER LANE,
FAZAKERLEY, LIVERPOOL, L9 7AL

COUNCIL OFFICE ☎ 0151 227 3911
MUNICIPAL BUILDINGS, DALE STREET,
LIVERPOOL, L69 2DH

STD Code 0161

Greater Manchester

MANCHESTER

MANCHESTER

100 0 400 yds
100 0 400 m

BBC RADIO GMR 95.1 FM
PICCADILLY GOLD 1152 AM, FORTUNE 1458 AM, KISS 102 FM, PICCADILLY KEY 103 FM

LOCAL RADIO

TOURIST INFORMATION ☎ 0161 234 3157/8
MANCHESTER VISITOR CENTRE, TOWN HALL
EXTENSION, LLOYD ST, MANCHESTER, M60 2LA

HOSPITAL A & E ☎ 0161 276 1234
MANCHESTER ROYAL INFIRMARY,
OXFORD ROAD, MANCHESTER, M13 9WL

COUNCIL OFFICE ☎ 0161 234 5000
TOWN HALL, ALBERT SQUARE,
MANCHESTER, M60 2LA

HARTLEPOOL
Historic Quay & Museum of Hartlepool
Seaton Carew
Tees Bay
Seal Sands
Tees Mouth
B1277
A178
Dalton Piercy
Elwick
A19
Greatham
A689
Newton Bewley
Cowpen Bewley
A185
A1046
Cargo Fleet
Port Clarence
Haverton Hill
Billingham
Wolviston
Wynyard
Castle Eden Walkway
Thorpe Thewles
Redmarshall
Carlton
Whitton
Thorpe Larches
Stillington
Bishopton
Little Stainton
Sadberge
Sadberge
A177
Foxton
Elstob
Mordon
Great Stainton
Coatham Mundeville

REDCAR
Coatham
Warrenby
Dormanstown
A1085
A1042
Kirkleatham
Kirkleatham Old Hall Mus
A1085
A174
Yearby
Wilton
Upleatham
New Marske
Marske-by-the-Sea
Saltburn-by
Brotton
SKELTON
Skelton
North Skelton
Skelton Green
Boosbeck
A173
A171
A1269
Dunsdale
Guisborough
Pinchinthorpe
Margrove Park
Lingdale
Stanghow
Moo
Moorsholm Moor
Warsett Hill
Carlin

A17
Danby L
Castleton
Westerdale
Baysdale Beck
Boysdale Beck
Freebrough Hill 329
Commondale Moor
Commondale
Gisborough Moor
Newton under Roseberry
Roseberry Topping 320
Easby Moor 324
Little Ayton
Kildale Moor
Kildale
Battersby
Ingleby Greenhow
Great Broughton
Great Ayton
Easby
A172
A173

GRANGETOWN
Georgetown
Grangetown
Lazenby
ESTON
Normanby
Eston
South Bank
A171
A66
Ormesby
Warren Field
Munthorpe
Coulby Newham
Newby
Tanton
Seamer
A172
STOKESLEY
A1365
B1365
Stokesley

MIDDLESBROUGH
Ormesby
A172
Acklam
A1032
Marton
Cook Birthplace Museum
Suzy Project
A19
Linthorpe
Hemlington
Stainton
Maltby
High Leven
Hilton
Thornaby-on-Tees
Preston Hall Museum
Ingleby Barwick
Eaglescliffe
Yarm
Aislaby
A135
A1044
Middleton on Leven
Crathorne
Hutton Rudby
Rudby
Sexhow
Enterpen
A19
A67
Picton

STOCKTON-ON-TEES
Hartburn
Elton
Urlay Nook
Allens West Sta.
Longnewton
A66
A67
Teesside Airport Sta.
Middleton St George
Middleton One Row
Low Dinsdale
Neasham
Eryholme
Low Worsall
Girsby
Sockburn
Low Entercommon
Appleton
Hurworth-on-Tees
A167

DARLINGTON
A1150
Great Burdon
Barmpton
Haughton Le Skerne
Eastbourne
A167
Hurworth Place

A1(M)
Newton Aycliffe
Aycliffe
Chilton
Rushyford
Bradbury
Brafferton
Coatham Mundeville

Ferryhill
Bishop Middleham
Hardwick Hall
A177
Fishburn
Sedgefield
B1278
B1277
A689

Tees
Leven
A67
A19
A171
A174
A172

MIDDLESBROUGH

STD Code 01642

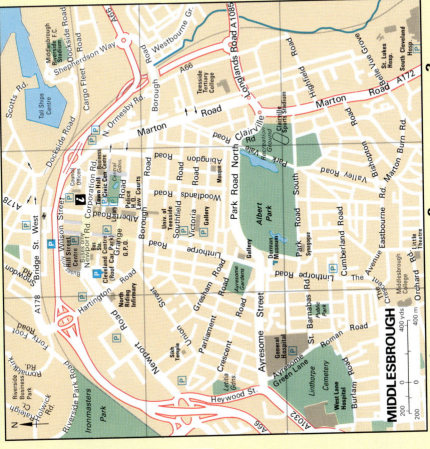

LOCAL RADIO

BBC RADIO CLEVELAND 95 FM
GREAT NORTH RADIO 1170 AM, TFM 96.6 FM, CENTURY RADIO 107.9 FM

TOURIST INFORMATION ☎ 01642 243425
51 CORPORATION ROAD,
MIDDLESBROUGH, TS1 1LT

HOSPITAL A & E ☎ 01642 617617
NORTH TEES GENERAL HOSPITAL, HARDWICK
ROAD, STOCKTON-0N-TEES, TS19 8PE

COUNCIL OFFICE ☎ 01642 245432
MUNICIPAL BUILDINGS, PO BOX 99A,
RUSSELL STREET, MIDDLESBROUGH, TS1 2QQ

STD Code 0191

Tyne & Wear

NEWCASTLE

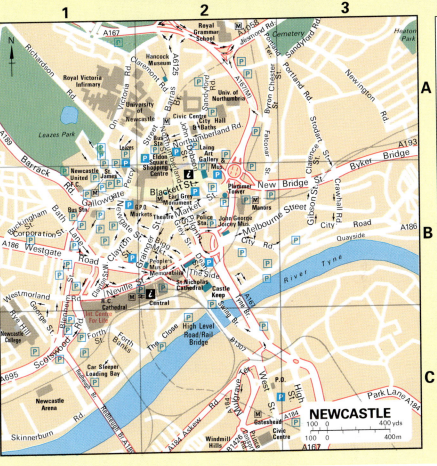

BBC RADIO NEWCASTLE 95.4 FM
GREAT NORTH RADIO 1152 AM, METRO FM 97.1 FM, CENTURY RADIO 101.8 FM

LOCAL RADIO

Askew Road	C2	Corporation Street	B1	Mulgrave Terrace	C2	Richardson Road	A1
Barrack Road	A1	Crawhall Road	B3	Neville Street	B1	Rye Hill	B1
Barras Bridge	A2	Dean Street	B2	New Bridge	B2	Sandyford Road	A2
Bath Lane	B1	Falconar Street	A2	Newgate Street	B1	Scotswood Road	C1
Bigg Market	B2	Forth Banks	C1	Newington Road	A3	Skinnerburn Road	C1
Blackett Street	B2	Gallowgate	B1	Northumberland Road	A2	Stodart Street	A3
Blenheim Street	C1	George Street	B1	Park Lane	C3	Swing Bridge	B2
Buckingham Street	B1	Gibson Street	B3	Percy Street	B1	The Close	C2
Byker Bridge	B3	Grainger Street	B2	Pilgrim Street	B2	The Side	B2
Byron Street	A2	Grey Street	B2	Prince Consort Road	C2	Tyne Bridge	B2
Chester Street	A2	High Street	C3	Portland Road	A3	West Street	C2
City Road	B2	Jesmond Road	A2	Portland Terrace	A2	Westgate Road	B1
Claremont Road	A1	John Dobson Street	A2	Quayside	B3	Westmorland Road	B1
Clarence Street	B3	Market Street	B2	Queen Victoria Road	A1		
Clayton Street	B1	Melbourne Street	B2	Redheugh Bridge	C1		

TOURIST INFORMATION ☎ 0191 261 0610
CENTRAL LIBRARY, PRINCESS SQ, NEWCASTLE-
UPON-TYNE, TYNE & WEAR, NE99 1DX

HOSPITAL A & E ☎ 0191 232 5131
ROYAL VICTORIA INFIRMARY, QUEEN VICTORIA
ROAD, NEWCASTLE-UPON-TYNE, NE1 4LP

COUNCIL OFFICE ☎ 0191 232 8520
CIVIC CENTRE, BARRAS BRIDGE,
NEWCASTLE-UPON-TYNE, NE99 2BN

NORWICH

Wymondham

Attleborough

Heath, Pott, Beig, Bastwick, Rollesby, Filby, Thrigby, Clippesby, Repps, Burgh St Margaret, Billockby, Stokesby, Tunstall, Moulton St Mary, Freethorpe, Wickhampton, Halvergate, Reedham, Lower Thurlton, Thurlton, Thorpe, Raveningham, Maypole Gr, Ludham, Upper Street, Thurne, Acle, Damgate, North Burlingham, Lingwood, South Burlingham, Southwood, Limpenhoe, Cantley, Hardley Street, Chedgrave, Heckingham, Hales, Kirby Cane, Catfield, Irstead, Neatishead, Horning, Woodbastwick, South Walsham, Hemblington, Strumpshaw, Buckenham, Hassingham, Beighton, Hales Hall, The Laurels, Loddon, Mundham, Sisland, Kirstead Green, Seething, Brooke, Howe, Shotesham, Saxlingham Nethergate, Hempnall, Barton, Turf, Barton Broad, Lawrence, Ashmanhaugh, Wroxham, Hoveton, Salhouse, Rackheath, Little Plumstead, Great Plumstead, Blofield, Brundall, Postwick, Surlingham, Bramerton, Rockland St Mary, Claxton, Ashby St Mary, Thurton, Bergh Apton, Langley Street, Alpington, Yelverton, Poringland, Sco Street, Tunstead, Ruston, Little Hautbois, Coltishall, Belaugh, Horstead, Crostwick, New Rackheath, Thorpe End Garden Village, Thorpe St Andrew, Kirby Bedon, Framingham Pigot, Framingham Earl, Stoke Holy Cross, Caistor St Edmund, Dunston, Saxlingham Thorpe, Saxlingham Green, Buxton, Stratton Strawless, Hainford, Frettenham, Newton St Faith, Horsham St Faith, Spixworth, Catton, Sprowston, Norwich, Towse Newton, Arminghall, Swardeston, Swainsthorpe, Newton Flotman, Waterloo, Hevingham, Horsford, Drayton, Hellesdon, New Costessey, Earlham, Eaton, Cringleford, Keswick, Intwood, East Carleton, Mulbarton, Bracon Ash, Flordon, Tasburgh, Heath, Felthorpe, St Helena, Ringland, Taverham, Costessey, Bowthorpe, Colney, Little Melton, Hethersett, Ketteringham, Ashwellthorpe, Wreningham, Hapton, Forncett St Mary, Tacolneston, Tharston, Swannington, Attlebridge, Weston Longville, Weston Green, Honingham, Easton, Marlingford, Bawburgh, Great Melton, High Green, Wramplingham, Barford, Silfield, Morley St Botolph, Suton, Spooner Row, Bunwell Street, Alderford, Morton, Colton, Barnham Broom, Kimberley, Crownthorpe, Wicklewood, Deopham, Brandon Parva, Runhall, Barnham Broom, Whitwell, Brandiston, Bawdeswell, Sparham, Lyng, Lenwade, Primrose Green, Elsing, Woodgate, Mill Street, Mattishall, North Tuddenham, Hockering, Mattishall Burgh, East Tuddenham, South Green, Welborne, Clint Green, Hackford, Coston, Barnham, Runhall, Thuxton, Hardingham, Deopham Green, Besthorpe, Foxley

A149, A1062, A1064, B1152, A140, A1042, A1151, A1067, A1074, A47, A11, A146, A143, A1149, B1150, B1140, B1354, B1149, B1145, B1108, B1172, B1135, B1332, B1136, B114

STD Code 01603 · Norfolk · NORWICH

NORWICH

400 yds / 400 m

LOCAL RADIO

BBC RADIO NORFOLK 95.1 FM
AMBER RADIO 1152 AM, RADIO BROADLAND 102.4 FM

TOURIST INFORMATION ☎ 01603 666071
THE GUILDHALL, GAOL HILL, NORWICH, NORFOLK, NR2 1NF

HOSPITAL A & E ☎ 01603 286286
NORFOLK & NORWICH HOSPITAL, BRUNSWICK ROAD, NORWICH, NR1 3SR

COUNCIL OFFICE ☎ 01603 622233
CITY HALL, ST. PETER'S STREET, NORWICH, NR2 1NH

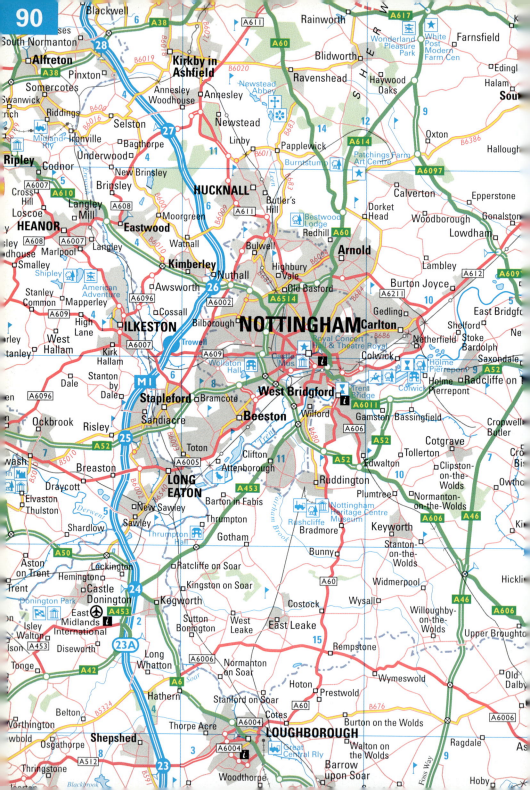

STD Code 0115

NOTTINGHAM

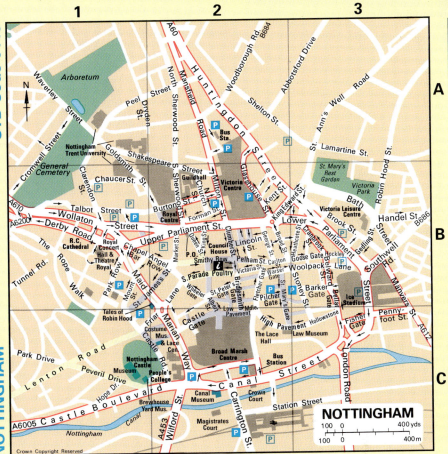

BBC RADIO NOTTINGHAM 95.5 FM
GEM AM 999 AM, TRENT FM 96.2 FM

LOCAL RADIO

TOURIST INFORMATION ☎ 0115 915 5330
1-4 SMITHY ROW, NOTTINGHAM,
NOTTINGHAMSHIRE, NG1 2BY

HOSPITAL A & E ☎ 0115 924 9924
QUEENS MEDICAL CENTRE, UNIVERSITY HOSP,
DERBY ROAD, NOTTINGHAM, NG7 2UH

COUNCIL OFFICE ☎ 0115 915 5555
THE GUILDHALL, BURTON STREET,
NOTTINGHAM, NG1 4BT

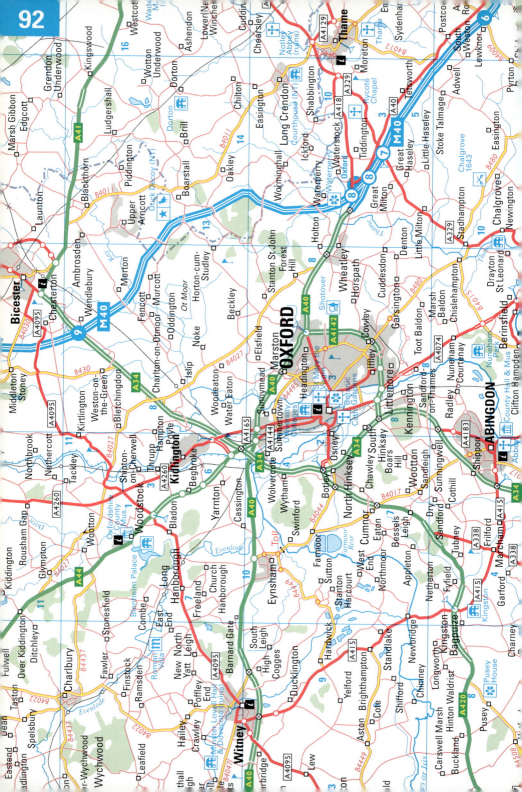

STD Code 01865

Oxfordshire

OXFORD

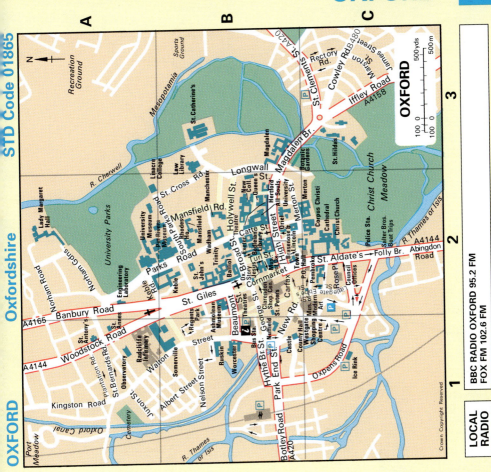

Abingdon Road	C2	Marston Street	C3
Albert Street	B1	Merton Street	B2
Banbury Road	A2	Nelson Street	B1
Beaumont Street	B1	New Road	B1
Botley Road	B1	Norham Gardens	A2
Broad Street	B2	Norham Road	A2
Cattle Street	B2	Oxpens Road	C1
Cornmarket	B2	Park End Street	B1
Cowley Road	C3	Parks Road	A2
Folly Bridge	C2	Plantation Road	A1
George Street	B1	Rectory Road	C3
High Street	B2	Rose Place	C2
Holywell Street	B2	St. Aldate's	C2
Hythe Bridge Street	B1	St. Bernards Road	A1
Iffley Road	C3	St. Clements Street	C3
James Street	C3	St. Cross Road	B2
Juxon Street	A1	St. Ebbe's Street	C2
Keble Road	A2	St. Giles	B2
Kingston Road	A1	South Parks Road	B2
Littlegate Street	C2	Turl Street	B2
Longwall Street	B3	Walton Street	B1
Magdalen Bridge	B3	Woodstock Road	A1
Mansfield Road	B2		

LOCAL RADIO
BBC RADIO OXFORD 95.2 FM
FOX FM 102.6 FM

TOURIST INFORMATION ☎ 01865 726871
THE OLD SCHOOL, GLOUCESTER GREEN,
OXFORD, OXFORDSHIRE, OX1 2DA

HOSPITAL A & E ☎ 01865 741166
JOHN RADCLIFFE HOSPITAL, HEADLEY WAY,
HEADINGTON, OXFORD, OX3 9DU

COUNCIL OFFICE ☎ 01865 249811
COUNCIL OFFICES, ST. ALDATES CHAMBERS,
OXFORD, OX1 1DS

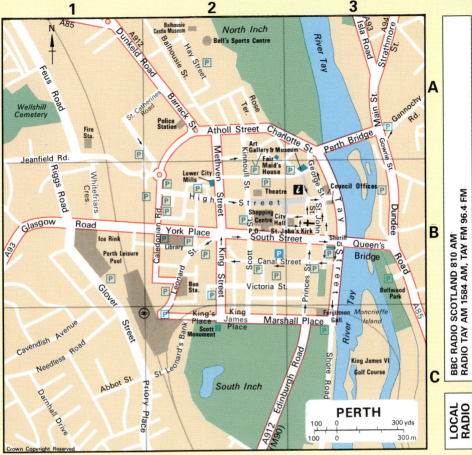

STD Code 01738

Perth & Kinross

PERTH

BBC RADIO SCOTLAND 810 AM
RADIO TAY AM 1584 AM, TAY FM 96.4 FM

LOCAL RADIO

PERTH

Abbot Street	C1	Feus Road	A1	King Street	B2	Rose Terrace	A2
Atholl Street	A2	Gannochy Road	A3	Kinnoull Street	A2	Scott Street	B2
Balhousie Street	A2	George Street	B3	Leonard Street	B2	Shore Road	C3
Barrack Street	A2	Glasgow Road	B1	Main Street	A3	South Street	B2
Caledonian Road	B2	Glover Street	B1	Marshall Place	C2	St. John Street	B3
Canal Street	B2	Gowrie Street	A3	Methven Street	A2	St. Leonard's Bank	C2
Cavendish Avenue	C1	Hay Street	A2	Needless Road	C1	Strathmore Street	A3
Charlotte Street	A2	High Street	B2	Perth Bridge	A3	Tay Street	B3
Darnhall Drive	C1	Isla Road	A3	Princes Street	B3	Victoria Street	B2
Dundee Road	B3	Jeanfield Road	A1	Priory Place	C2	York Place	B2
Dunkeld Road	A1	King's Place	C2	Queens Bridge	B3		
Edinburgh Road	C2	King James Place	C2	Riggs Road	B1		

TOURIST INFORMATION ☎ 01738 638353
45 HIGH STREET, PERTH, PH1 5TJ

HOSPITAL A & E ☎ 01738 623311
PERTH ROYAL INFIRMARY,
TAYMOUNT TERRACE, PERTH, PH1 1NX

COUNCIL OFFICE ☎ 01738 475000
PERTH & KINROSS COUNCIL, PO BOX 77,
2 HIGH STREET, PERTH, PH1 5PH

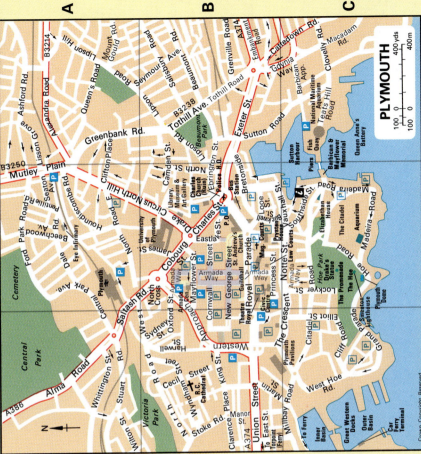

PLYMOUTH

Crown Copyright Reserved

TOURIST INFORMATION ☎ 01752 264849
ISLAND HOUSE, 9 THE BARBICAN, PLYMOUTH,
DEVON, PL1 2LS

HOSPITAL A & E ☎ 01752 777111
DERRIFORD HOSPITAL, DERRIFORD ROAD,
CROWNHILL, PLYMOUTH, PL6 8DH

COUNCIL OFFICE ☎ 01752 668000
CIVIC CENTRE, ARMADA WAY,
PLYMOUTH, PL1 2EW

LOCAL RADIO
BBC RADIO DEVON 103.4 FM
PLYMOUTH SOUND FM 97 FM

STD Code 01705

PORTSMOUTH

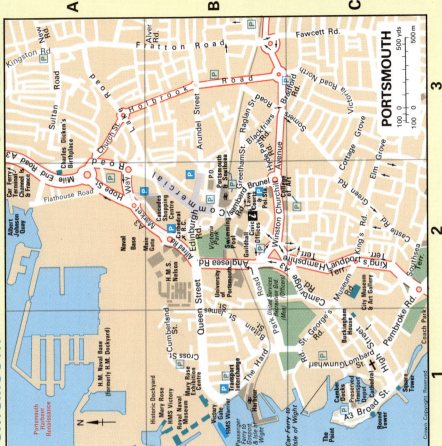

LOCAL RADIO
BBC RADIO SOLENT 96.1 FM
OCEAN FM 97.5 FM, SOUTH COAST RADIO 1170 AM

TOURIST INFORMATION ☎ 01705 826722
THE HARD, PORTSMOUTH, HAMPSHIRE, PO1 3QJ

HOSPITAL A & E ☎ 01705 286000
QUEEN ALEXANDRA HOSPITAL, SOUTHWICK HILL ROAD, COSHAM, PORTSMOUTH, PO6 3LY

COUNCIL OFFICE ☎ 01705 822251
CIVIC OFFICES, GUILDHALL SQUARE, PORTSMOUTH, PO1 2AL

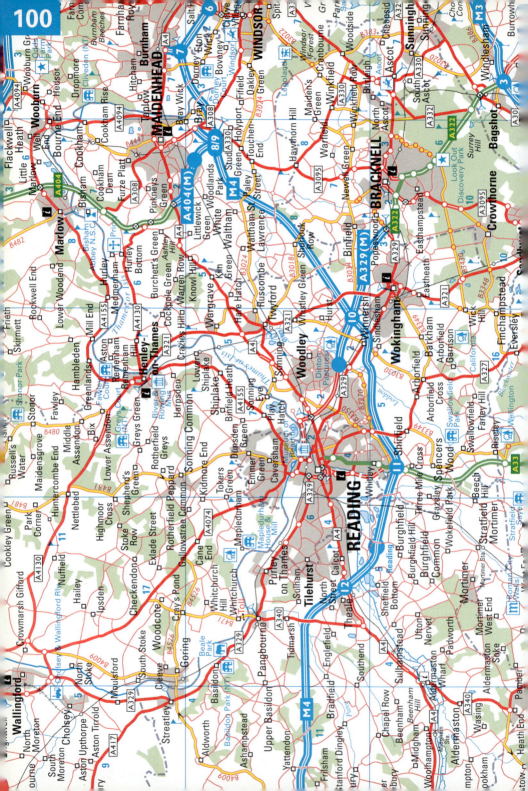

STD Code 0118

READING

BBC THAMES VALLEY RADIO 104.4 FM
CLASSIC GOLD 1431 1431 AM, 2-TEN FM 97 FM

LOCAL RADIO

Addington Road	C3
Alexandra Road	B3
Allcroft Road	C3
Ardler Road	A2
Bath Road	C1
Bedford Road	B1
Berkeley Avenue	C1
Blenheim Road	B3
Briant's Avenue	A3
Bridge Street	B2
Broad Street	B2
Cardiff Road	A1
Castle Hill	B1
Castle Street	B2
Caversham Road	B2
Chatham Street	B1
Cholmeley Road	B3
Christchurch Road	C2
Church Street	A1
Church Street	A2
Coley Avenue	C1
Craven Road	B3
Cumberland Road	B3
Duke Street	B2
East Street	B2
Eldon Road	B3
Elgar Road	C2
Elgar Road South	C2
Elmhurst Road	C3
Erleigh Road	C3
Field Road	B1
Forbury Road	B2
Friar Street	B2
George Street *Caversham*	A2
George Street *Reading*	B1

Gosbrook Road	A2
Great Knollys Street	B1
Henley Road	A2
Holybrook Road	C1
Kendrick Road	C2
King's Road	B2
London Road	B3
London Street	B2
Mill Lane	B2
Minster Street	B2
Morgan Road	C3
Orts Road	B3
Oxford Road	B1
Pell Street	C2
Prospect Street *Caversham*	A2
Prospect Street *Reading*	B1
Queen's Road	B2
Redlands Road	C3
Richfield Avenue	A1
Rose Kiln Lane	C2
Russell Street	B1
St. John's Road	A3
Southampton Street	C2
South View Avenue	A2
Station Road	B2
Tilehurst Road	B1
Upper Redlands Road	C3
Vastern Road	A2
Waterloo Road	C3
Watlington Street	B3
Western Elms Avenue	B1
West Street	B2
Whitley Street	C2

TOURIST INFORMATION ☎ **0118 956 6226**
TOWN HALL, BLAGRAVE STREET, READING,
BERKSHIRE, RG1 1QH

HOSPITAL A & E ☎ **0118 987 5111**
ROYAL BERKSHIRE HOSPITAL, LONDON ROAD,
READING, RG1 5AN

COUNCIL OFFICE ☎ **0118 939 0900**
CIVIC CENTRE, CIVIC OFFICES, (OFF CASTLE ST.)
READING, RG1 7TD

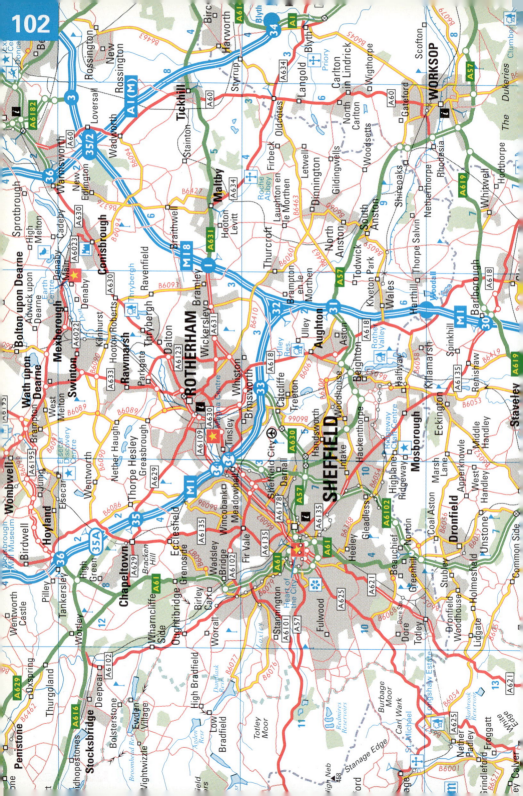

SHEFFIELD · **South Yorkshire** · **STD Code 0114**

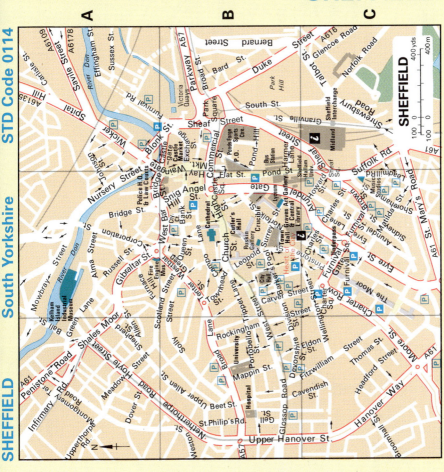

SHEFFIELD

Allen Street	A1	Furnace Hill	A2	Queen Street	B2
Alma Street	A2	Furnival Gate	C2	Rockingham Street	B1
Angel Street	B2	Furnival Road	A3	Russell Street	A2
Arundel Gate	C2	Furnival Square	C2	Savile Street	A3
Arundel Street	C2	Furnival Street	C2	Scotland Street	A1
Ball Street	A1	Gell Street	B1	Shales Moor	A1
Bank Street	B2	Gibraltar Street	A2	Sheaf Square	C2
Bard Street	B3	Glencoe Road	C3	Sheaf Street	C2
Barker's Pool	B1	Glossop Road	B1	Shepherd Street	A1
Beet Street	B1	Granville Street	C2	Shoreham Street	C2
Bernard Street	B3	Green Lane	A1	Shrewsbury Road	C3
Blonk Street	A2	Hanover Way	B1	Sidney Street	C2
Bridge Street	A2	Harmer Lane	C2	Snig Hill	B2
Broad Lane	A1	Haymarket	B2	Solly Street	B1
Broad Street	B3	Headford Street	B1	South Street	C2
Broomhall Street	C1	High Street	B2	Spital Hill	A3
Brown Street	C2	Howard Street	C2	St. Mary's Road	C2
Campo Lane	B2	Hoyle Street	A1	St. Philip's Road	B1
Carlisle Street	A3	Infirmary Road	A1	Suffolk Road	C2
Carver Street	B2	Johnson Street	A2	Surrey Street	B2
Castle Square	B2	Leadmill Road	C2	Sussex Street	A3
Castlegate	B3	Leopold Street	B2	Talbot Street	C3
Cavendish Street	B1	Mappin Street	B1	Tenter Street	B2
Charles Street	C2	Matilda Street	C2	The Moor	C1
Charter Row	C2	Meadow Street	A1	Thomas Street	B2
Charter Square	C2	Montgomery Terrace Road	A1	Townhead Street	B1
Church Street	B2	Moore Street	C1	Trippet Lane	B2
Commercial Street	B2	Mowbray Street	A2	Upper Allen Street	A1
Corporation Street	A2	Netherthorpe Road	B1	Upper Hanover Street	B1
Devonshire Street	B1	Norfolk Road	C3	Upperthorpe Road	A1
Division Street	B1	Norfolk Street	B2	Waingate	B3
Dover Street	A1	Nursery Street	A2	Wellington Street	C1
Duke Street	B3	Park Square	B3	West Bar	B2
Effingham Street	A3	Parkway	A3	West Street	B1
Eldon Street	C1	Penistone Road	A1	Westbar Green	B2
Exchange Street	B2	Pinstone Street	C2	Weston Street	B1
Eyre Lane	C2	Pond Hill	C2	Wicker	A3
Eyre Street	C2	Pond Street	B2		
Fitzwilliam Street	B1	Portobello Street	B1		
Flat Street	B2				

LOCAL RADIO

BBC RADIO SHEFFIELD 104.1 FM
HALLAM FM 97.4 FM, GREAT YORKSHIRE GOLD 1548 AM

TOURIST INFORMATION ☎ 0114 273 4671/2
PEACE GARDENS, SHEFFIELD,
SOUTH YORKSHIRE, S1 2HH

HOSPITAL A & E ☎ 0114 243 4343
NORTHERN GENERAL HOSPITAL, HERRIES ROAD,
SHEFFIELD, S5 7AU

COUNCIL OFFICE ☎ 0114 272 6444
TOWN HALL, PINSTONE STREET,
SHEFFIELD, S1 2HH

STD Code 01703

SOUTHAMPTON

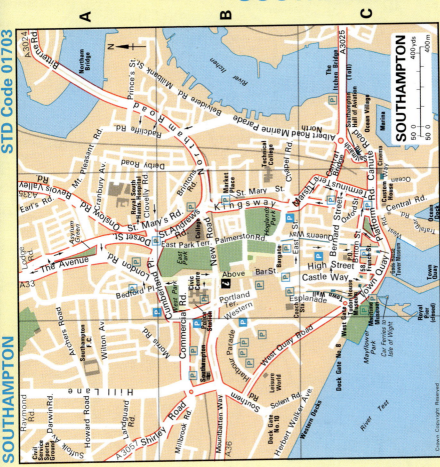

SOUTHAMPTON

400 yds
400 m
50   0
50   0

Crown Copyright Reserved

LOCAL RADIO

BBC RADIO SOLENT 96.1 FM
SOUTH COAST RADIO 1557 AM, POWER FM 103.2 FM

Above Bar Street	B2	Marsh Lane	B2
Albert Road North	C3	Millbank Street	B3
Archers Road	A1	Millbrook Road	B1
Bedford Place	A2	Morris Road	B1
Belvidere Road	B3	Mountbatten Way	A2
Bernard Street	C2	Mount Pleasant Road	B3
Bevois Valley Road	A2	New Road	B2
Bitterne Road	A3	Northam Road	B3
Brintons Road	B2	Ocean Way	C2
Briton Street	C2	Onslow Road	A2
Canute Road	C2	Oxford Street	C2
Castle Way	C2	Palmerston Road	B2
Central Bridge	C2	Platform Road	C2
Central Road	C2	Portland Terrace	B2
Chapel Road	B2	Prince's Street	A3
Clovelly Road	A2	Queen's Way	C2
Commercial Road	A2	Radcliffe Road	B1
Cranbury Avenue	A2	Raymond Road	A1
Cumberland Place	A2	St. Andrews Road	B2
Darwin Road	A1	St. Mary's Road	A2
Derby Road	B3	St. Mary Street	B2
Dorset Street	A2	Saltmarsh Road	C3
Earl's Road	A2	Shirley Road	A1
East Park Terrace	B2	Solent Road	B1
East Street	B2	Southern Road	B1
Herbert Walker Avenue	B1	Suffolk Avenue	A1
High Street	C2	Terminus Terrace	C2
Hill Lane	A1	The Avenue	A2
Howard Road	A1	Town Quay	C2
Kingsway	B2	Trafalgar Road	B1
Landguard Road	A1	West Quay Road	C2
Lodge Road	A2	West Road	C2
London Road	A2	Western Esplanade	B2
Marine Parade	B3	Wilton Avenue	A1

TOURIST INFORMATION ☎ 01703 221106
9 CIVIC CENTRE ROAD, SOUTHAMPTON,
HAMPSHIRE, SO14 7JP

HOSPITAL A & E ☎ 01703 777222
SOUTHAMPTON GENERAL HOSP, TREMONA RD,
SHIRLEY, SOUTHAMPTON, SO16 6YD

COUNCIL OFFICE ☎ 01703 223855
CIVIC CENTRE, CIVIC CENTRE ROAD,
SOUTHAMPTON, SO14 7LY

STD Code 01782

STOKE-ON-TRENT

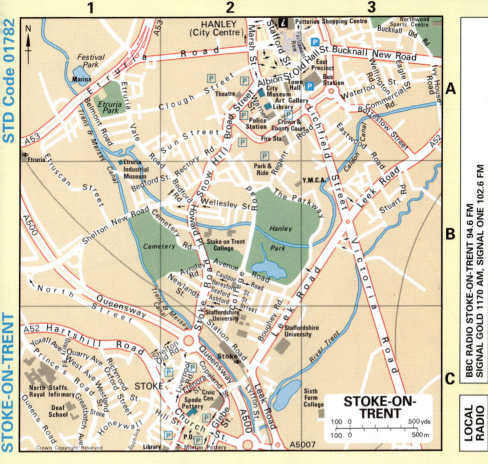

BBC RADIO STOKE-ON-TRENT 94.6 FM
SIGNAL GOLD 1170 AM, SIGNAL ONE 102.6 FM

LOCAL RADIO

Albion Street	A2	Clough Street	A2	Ivy House Road	A3	Shelton New Road	B1
Ashford Street	B2	College Road	C2	Leek Road	C2	Shelton Old Road	C1
Avenue Road	B2	Commercial Road	A3	Lichfield Street	A3	Snow Hill	B2
Aynsley Road	B2	Copeland Street	C2	Liverpool Road	C2	Stafford Street	A2
Bedford Road	B2	Eagle Street	A3	Lytton Street	C2	Station Road	C2
Bedford Street	B1	Eastwood Road	A3	Marsh Street	A2	Stoke	C2
Belmont Road	A1	Elenora Street	C2	Newlands Street	B2	Stoke Road	C2
Beresford Street	B2	Etruria Road	A1	North Street	B1	Stone	C1
Boon Avenue	C1	Etruria Vale Road	A1	Old Hall Street	A2	Stuart Road	B3
Botteslow Street	A3	Etruscan Street	A1	Oxford Street	C1	Sun Street	A2
Boughey Road	C2	Glebe Street	C2	Parliament Row	A2	The Parkway	B2
Broad Street	A2	Greatbatch Avenue	C1	Prince's Road	C1	Victoria Road	B3
Bucknall New Road	A3	Hanley	A2	Quarry Avenue	C1	Warner Street	A2
Bucknall Old Road	A3	Hartshill Road	C1	Quarry Road	C1	Waterloo Street	A3
Cauldon Road	B2	Hill Street	C2	Queen's Road	C1	Wellesley Street	B2
Cemetery Road	B1	Honeywall	C1	Queensway	B1	Wellington Road	A3
Church Street	C2	Howard Place	B2	Rectory Road	B2	West Avenue	C1
				Regent Road	B2	Westland Street	C1
				Richmond Street	C1	Yoxall Avenue	C1
				Seaford Street	B2		

TOURIST INFORMATION ☎ 01782 236000
POTTERIES SHOPPING CENTRE, QUADRANT RD,
STOKE-ON-TRENT, STAFFORDSHIRE, ST1 1RZ

HOSPITAL A & E ☎ 01782 715444
NORTH STAFFORDSHIRE ROYAL INFIRMARY,
PRINCE'S ROAD, STOKE-ON-TRENT, ST4 7LN

COUNCIL OFFICE ☎ 01782 234567
TOWN HALL, CIVIC CENTRE, GLEBE STREET,
STOKE-ON-TRENT, ST4 1HH

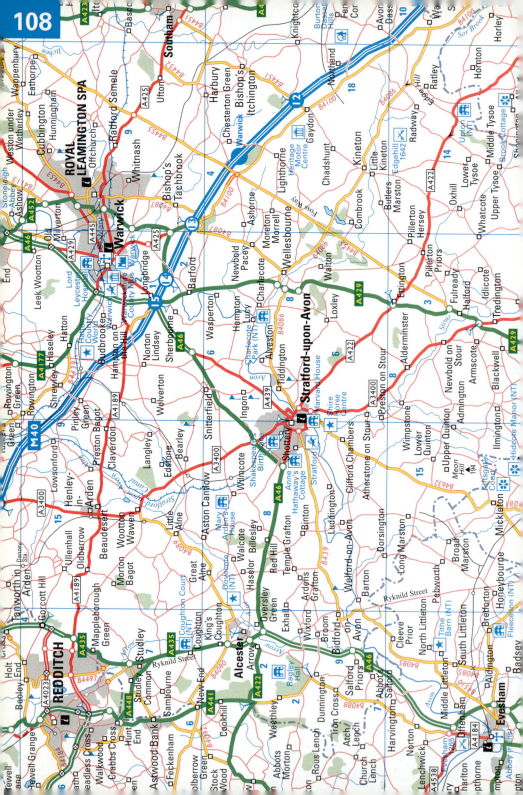

STRATFORD-UPON-AVON

STRATFORD-UPON-AVON Warwickshire STD Code 01789

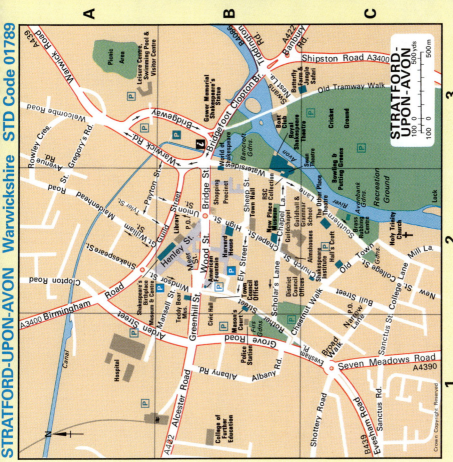

Albany Road	B1	Mansell Street	B1
Alcester Road	B1	Meer Street	B2
Arden Street	B1	Mill Lane	C2
Avenue Road	A3	Narrow Lane	C1
Banbury Road	B3	New Street	C2
Birmingham Road	A1	Old Town	C2
Bridgefoot	B2	Old Tramway Walk	C3
Bridge Street	B2	Payton Street	A2
Bridgeway	B3	Rother Street	B1
Broad Walk	C1	Rowley Crescent	A3
Bull Street	C2	St. Gregory's Road	A2
Chapel Lane	B2	Sanctus Road	C1
Chapel Street	B2	Sanctus Street	C1
Chestnut Walk	B1	Scholar's Lane	B2
Church Street	C2	Shakespeare Street	A2
Clopton Bridge	B3	Sheep Street	B2
Clopton Road	A2	Shipston Road	C3
College Lane	C2	Shottery Road	B1
College Street	C2	Seven Meadows Road	C1
Ely Street	C1	Southern Lane	C2
Evesham Place	C1	Swans Nest lane	B3
Evesham Road	B1	Tiddington Road	B3
Great William Street	A2	Union Street	B2
Greenhill Street	B1	Warwick Road	B2
Grove Road	B1	Waterside	B2
Guild Street	B2	Welcombe Road	A3
Henley Street	B2	Windsor Street	B2
High Street	B2	Wood Street	B2
Maidenhead Road	A2		

LOCAL RADIO

BBC RADIO CWR 94.8 & 103.7 FM
THE BEAR 102 FM

TOURIST INFORMATION ☎ 01789 293127
BRIDGEFOOT, STRATFORD-UPON-AVON,
WARWICKSHIRE, CV37 6GW

HOSPITAL A & E ☎ 01789 205831
STRATFORD-UPON-AVON HOSPITAL, ARDEN ST,
STRATFORD-UPON-AVON, CV37 6NX

COUNCIL OFFICE ☎ 01789 267575
COUNCIL OFFICES, ELIZABETH HOUSE,
CHURCH ST, STRATFORD-UPON-AVON, CV37 6HX

STD Code 01792

SWANSEA

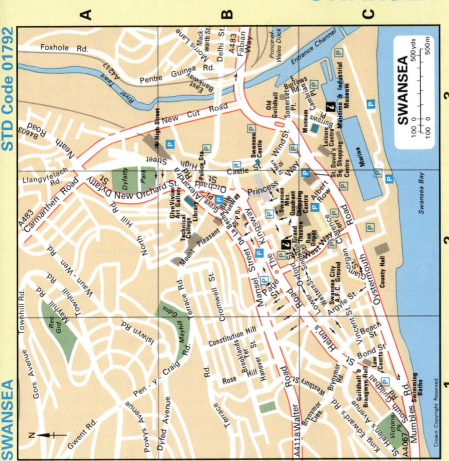

Albert Row	C2
Alexandra Road	B2
Argyle Street	C2
Beach Street	C1
Belle Vue Way	B2
Bond Street	C1
Brooklands Terrace	B1
Brynymor Crescent	C1
Brynymor Road	B1
Burrows Place	C3
Cambrian Place	C3
Carmarthen Road	A2
Castle Street	B2
Clarence Terrace	C2
Constitution Hill	B1
Cromwell Street	B2
De La Beche Street	B2
Delhi Street	B1
Dylatty Street	A2
Dyfed Avenue	B1
East Bankway	B3
East Burrows Road	B3
Fabian Way	B3
Glamorgan Street	C2
Gors Avenue	A3
Grove Place	A1
Gwent Road	B2
Hanover Street	C1
High Street	B3
Islwyn Road	A1
King Edward's Road	C1
Llangyfelach Road	A2
Lower Oxford Street	B3

Mackworth Street	B3
Mansel Street	B2
Mayhill Road	A1
Morris Lane	B3
Mount Pleasant	B2
Mumbles Road	C1
Neath Road	A3
New Cut Road	B3
New Orchard Street	A2
North Hill Road	A2
Orchard Street	B2
Oystermouth Road	C2
Page Street	B2
Pentre Guinea Road	A3
Pen-y-Craig Road	C2
Powys Avenue	A1
Princess Way	B2
Rose Hill	B1
St. Helen's Avenue	C1
St. Helen's Road	C1
St. Mary Street	B2
Singleton Street	C2
Somerset Place	B3
South Guildhall Road	C1
Terrace Road	B1
The Kingsway	B2
Townhill Road	A2
Vincent Street	C1
Walter Road	B1
Waun-Wen Road	A2
Westbury Street	C1
Western Street	C2
West Way	A2
Wind Street	B3

LOCAL RADIO
BBC RADIO WALES 882 AM
SWANSEA SOUND 1170 AM, SOUND WAVE 96.4 96.4 FM

TOURIST INFORMATION ☎ 01792 468321
WEST WAY CAR PARK, SWANSEA, SA1 3QG

HOSPITAL A & E ☎ 01792 702222
MORRISTON HOSPITAL, MORRISTON, SWANSEA, SA6 6NL

COUNCIL OFFICE ☎ 01792 636000
THE GUILDHALL, (OFF FRANCIS STREET), SWANSEA, SA1 4PA

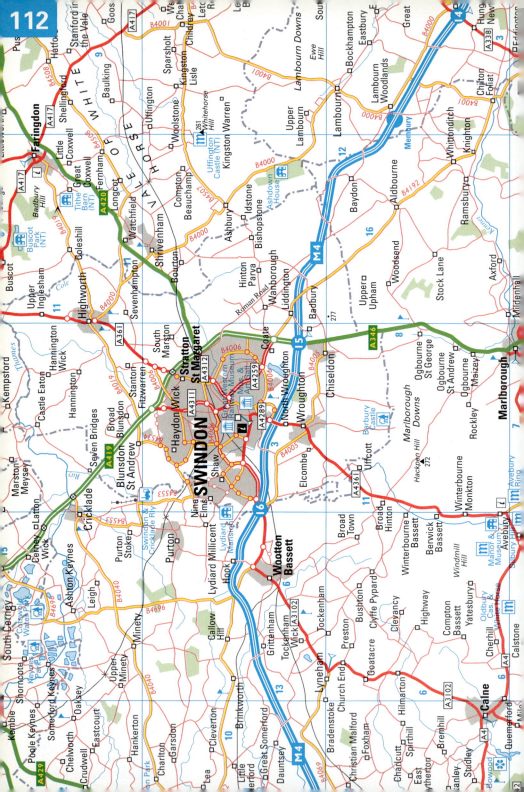

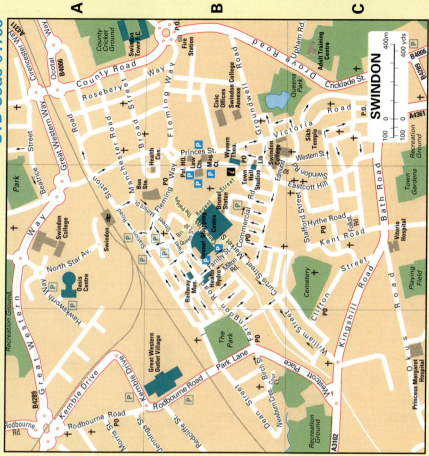

STD Code 01793

SWINDON

Index

Bath Road	C2
Beatrice Street	A2
Birch Street	B1
Bridge Street	B2
Broad Street	A3
Canal Walk	B2
Cirencester Way	A3
Clifton Street	C1
Commercial Road	B2
County Road	A3
Courtsknap Court	B1
Cricklade Street	C3
Curtis Street	B2
Dean Street	B1
Drove Road	C3
Eastcott Hill	C2
Edmund Street	B2
Faringdon Road	B1
Farnby Street	B2
Fleet Street	B2
Fleming Way	C2
Folkstone Road	A1
Great Western Way	B3
Groundwell Road	A1
Hawksworth Way	C2
Hythe Road	B1
Jennings Street	A1
Kemble Drive	
Kent Road	C2
Kingshill Road	C1
Manchester Road	A2
Market Street	B2
Milford Street	B2
Milton Road	B2
Morris Street	A1
Newburn Crescent	B1
North Star Avenue	A2
Ocotal Way	A3
Okus Road	C1
Park Lane	B3
Princes Street	B2
Queen Street	B1
Redcliffe Street	B2
Regent Street	A1
Rodbourne Road	A3
Rosebery Way	A2
Stafford Street	C2
Station Road	B2
Swindon Road	C3
The Parade	B3
Upham Road	C1
Victoria Road	C3
Westcott Place	C1
Western Street	C3
William Street	C10

LOCAL RADIO

BBC WILTSHIRE SOUND 103.6 FM
GWR FM 97.2 FM

TOURIST INFORMATION ☎ 01793 530328
37 REGENT STREET, SWINDON, SN1 1JL

HOSPITAL A & E ☎ 01793 536231
PRINCESS MARGARET HOSPITAL, OKUS ROAD,
SWINDON, SN1 4JU

COUNCIL OFFICE ☎ 01793 463000
CIVIC OFFICES, EUCLID STREET, SWINDON,
SN1 2JH

STD Code 01803

Torbay

TORQUAY

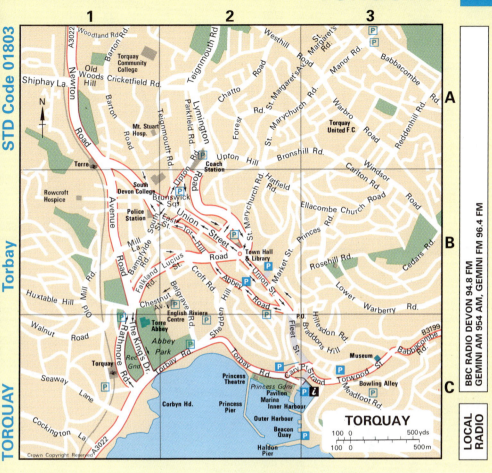

BBC RADIO DEVON 94.8 FM
GEMINI AM 954 AM, GEMINI FM 96.4 FM

LOCAL RADIO

Abbey Road	B2	Croft Road	B2	Mill Lane	B1	Strand	C3
Avenue Road	B1	East Street	B2	Newton Road	A1	Teignmouth Road	A2
Babbacombe Road	C3	Ellacombe Church		Old Mill Road	B1	The King's Drive	C1
Bampfylde Road	B1	Road	B3	Old Woods Hill	A1	Torbay Road	C2
Barton Road	A1	Falkland Road	B1	Parkfield Road	A2	Tor Hill Road	B2
Belgrave Road	B2	Fleet Street	C2	Prince's Road	B3	Torwood Street	C3
Braddons Hill	C3	Forest Road	A2	Rathmore Road	C1	Union Street	B2
Bronshill Road	A2	Hatfield Road	B2	Reddenhill Road	A3	Upton Hill	A2
Brunswick Square	B2	Hillesdon Road	C3	Rosehill Road	B3	Upton Road	B2
Carlton Road	A3	Huxtable Hill	B1	St. Margaret's Avenue	A2	Walnut Road	C1
Cary Parade	C2	Lower Warberry Road	B3	St. Margaret's Road	A3	Warbro Road	A3
Cedars Road	B3	Lucius Street	B2	St. Marychurch Road	B2	Westhill Road	A2
Chatto Road	A2	Lymington Road	A2	Seaway Lane	C1	Windsor Road	B3
Chestnut Avenue	B1	Manor Road	A3	Shedden Hill	C2		
Cockington Lane	C1	Market Street	B2	Shiphay Lane	A1		
Cricketfield Road	A1	Meadfoot Road	C3	South Street	B1		

TOURIST INFORMATION ☎ 01803 297428
VAUGHAN PARADE, TORQUAY, DEVON, TQ2 5JG

HOSPITAL A & E ☎ 01803 614567
TORBAY DISTRICT GENERAL HOSPITAL,
LAWES BRIDGE, TORQUAY, TQ2 7AA

COUNCIL OFFICE ☎ 01803 296244
CIVIC OFFICES, CASTLE CIRCUS,
TORQUAY, TQ1 3DR

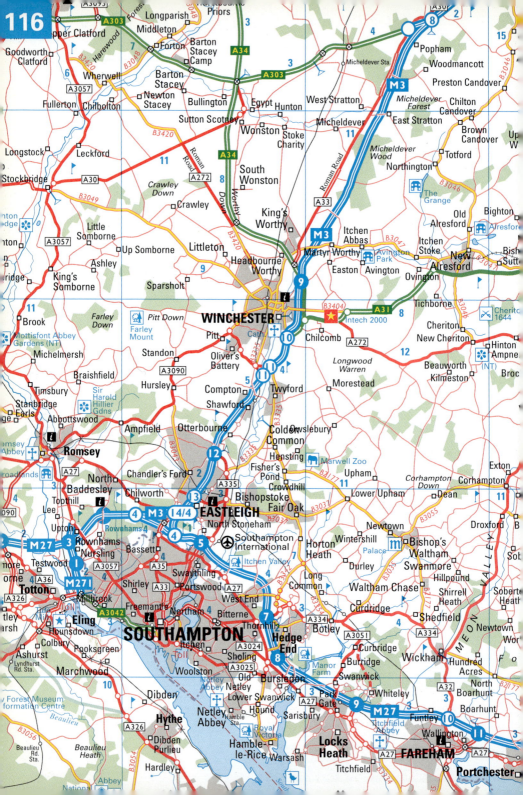

STD Code 01962

Hampshire

WINCHESTER

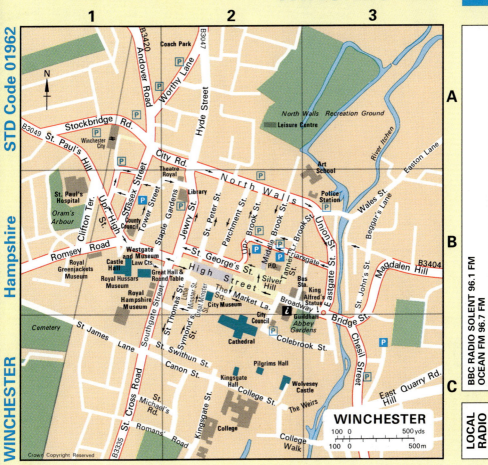

WINCHESTER

100 0   500 yds
100 0   500 m

Crown Copyright Reserved

BBC RADIO SOLENT 96.1 FM
OCEAN FM 96.7 FM

LOCAL RADIO

TOURIST INFORMATION ☎ 01962 840500
GUILDHALL, THE BROADWAY, WINCHESTER
HAMPSHIRE, SO23 9LJ

HOSPITAL A & E ☎ 01962 863535
ROYAL HAMPSHIRE COUNTY HOSPITAL,
ROMSEY ROAD, WINCHESTER, SO22 5DG

COUNCIL OFFICE ☎ 01962 840222
CITY OFFICES, COLEBROOK STREET,
WINCHESTER, SO23 9LJ

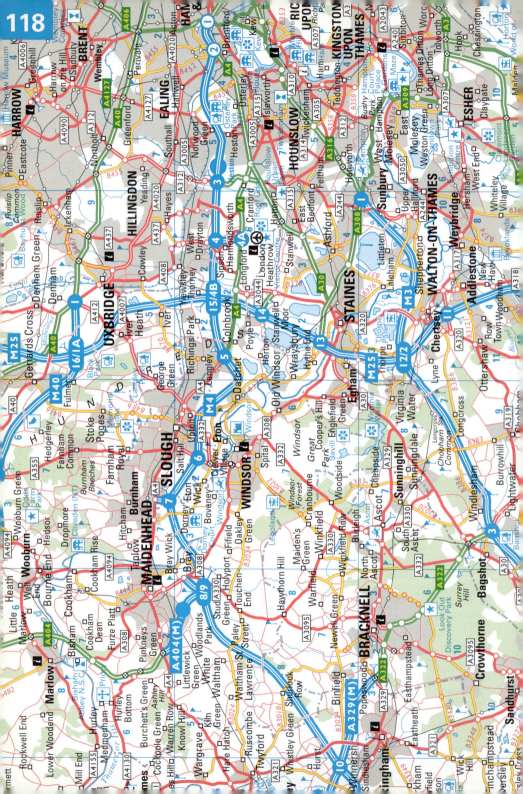

WINDSOR Windsor & Maidenhead STD Code 01753

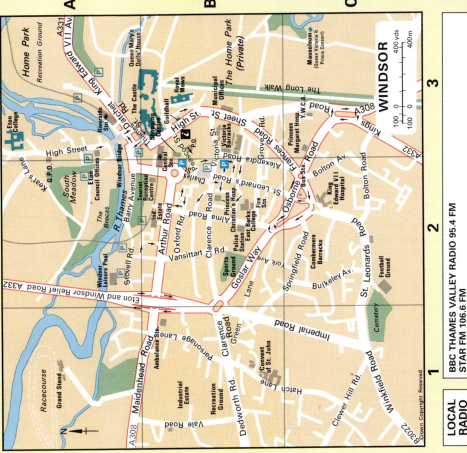

LOCAL RADIO
BBC THAMES VALLEY RADIO 95.4 FM
STAR FM 106.6 FM

Street	Grid
Alexandra Road	B2
Alma Road	B2
Arthur Road	B2
Barry Avenue	A2
Bolton Avenue	C2
Bolton Road	C2
Bulkeley Avenue	B2
Charles Street	B2
Clarence Road	B1
Clewer Hill Road	C1
Datchet Road	A3
Dedworth Road	B1
Eton & Windsor Relief Road	A2
Frances Road	C2
Goslar Way	B2
Green Lane	B1
Grove Road	B3
Hatch Lane	C1
High Street (Eton)	A3
High Street (Windsor)	B3

Street	Grid
Imperial Road	C1
Keat's Lane	A2
King Edward VII Avenue	A3
Kings Road	C3
Maidenhead Road	A1
Osborne Road	C2
Oxford Road	B2
Parsonage Lane	B1
Peascod Street	B2
St. Leonards Road	C2
Sheet Street	B3
Springfield Road	C2
Stovell Road	A2
Thames Street	B3
The Long Walk	C3
Vale Road	B1
Vansittart Road	B2
Victoria Street	B2
Winkfield Road	C1
York Avenue	B2

TOURIST INFORMATION ☎ 01753 852010
24 HIGH STREET, WINDSOR, BERKSHIRE, SL4 1LH

HOSPITAL A & E ☎ 01753 633000
WEXHAM PARK HOSPITAL, WEXHAM STREET,
SLOUGH, SL2 4HL

COUNCIL OFFICE ☎ 01753 810525
COUNCIL OFFICES, YORK HOUSE,
SHEET STREET, WINDSOR, SL4 1DD

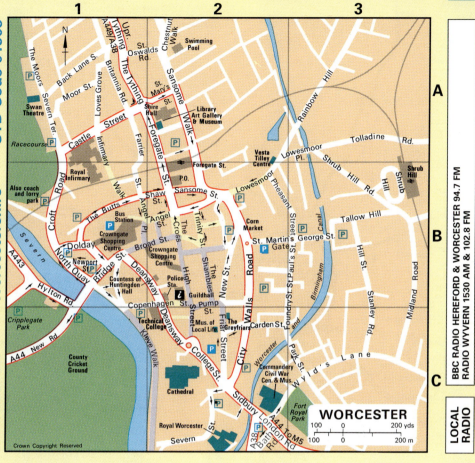

STD Code 01905

Worcestershire

WORCESTER

BBC RADIO HEREFORD & WORCESTER 94.7 FM
RADIO WYVERN 1530 AM & 102.8 FM

LOCAL RADIO

Angel Place	B1	Farrier Street	A1	Newport Street	B1	Shaw Street	B2
Angel Street	B2	Foregate Street	A2	New Road	C1	Shrub Hill	B3
Back Lane South	A1	Foundry Street	C3	New Street	B2	Shrub Hill Road	A3
Bath Road	C2	Friar Street	C2	North Quay	B1	Sidbury	C2
Bridge Street	B1	George Street	B3	Park Street	C3	Stanley Road	B3
Britannia Road	A1	High Street	B2	Pheasant Street	B2	Tallow Hill	B3
Broad Street	B1	Hill Street	B3	Pump Street	B2	The Butts	B1
Carden Street	C2	Hylton Road	B1	Rainbow Hill	A3	The Cross	B2
Castle Street	A1	Infirmary Walk	A1	St. Martin's Gate	B2	The Moors	A1
Chestnut Walk	A2	Kleve Walk	C1	St. Mary's Street	A2	The Shambles	B2
City Walls Road	C2	London Road	C2	St. Oswalds Road	A1	The Tything	A1
College Street	C2	Loves Grove	A1	St. Paul's Street	B3	Tolladine Road	A3
Copenhagen Street	B1	Lowesmoor	B2	Sansome Street	B2	Trinity Street	B2
Croft Road	B1	Lowesmoor Place	A2	Sansome Walk	A2	Upper Tything	A1
Deansway	B1	Midland Road	C3	Severn Street	C2	Wyld's Lane	C3
Dolday	B1	Moor Street	A1	Severn Terrace	A1		

TOURIST INFORMATION ☎ 01905 726311
THE GUILDHALL, HIGH STREET,
WORCESTER, WR1 2EY

HOSPITAL A & E ☎ 01905 763333
WORCESTER ROYAL INFIRMARY, RONKSWOOD
BRANCH, NEWTOWN ROAD, WR5 1HN

COUNCIL OFFICE ☎ 01905 723471
GUILDHALL, HIGH STREET,
WORCESTER, WR1 2EY

STD Code 01904

YORK

YORK

100 0 400m
100 0 400 yds

BBC RADIO YORK 103.7 FM
MINSTER FM 104.7 FM

LOCAL RADIO

Albemarle Road	C1	East Parade	A3	Lawrence Street	C3	Piccadilly	B2
Aldwark	B2	Fifth Avenue	A3	Layerthorpe	B3	Queen Street	B1
Barbican Road	C3	Fishergate	C2	Leeman Road	B1	Rougier Street	B1
Bishopthorpe Road	C2	Foss Bank	B3	Lendal	B2	St. Andrewgate	B2
Bishopgate Street	C2	Fossgate	B2	Lord Mayor's Walk	A2	St. John's Street	A2
Blossom Street	C1	Foss Islands Road	B3	Lowther Street	A2	St. Maurice's Road	B2
Bootham	A1	Fourth Avenue	B3	Malton Road	A3	Scarcroft Hill	C1
Bull Lane	A3	Gillygate	A2	Micklegate	B1	Scarcroft Road	C1
Burton Stone Lane	A1	Goodramgate	B2	Monkgate	A2	Shambles	B2
Cemetery Road	C3	Grosvenor Road	A1	Moss Street	C1	Sixth Avenue	A3
Church Street	B2	Grosvenor Terrace	A1	Museum Street	B2	Skeldergate	B2
Clarence Street	A2	Hallfield Road	B3	North Street	B2	Southlands Road	C1
Clifford Street	B2	Haxby Road	A2	Nunnery Lane	C1	Station Road	B1
Clifton	A1	Heslington Road	C3	Nunthorpe Road	C1	Tadcaster Road	C1
Coney Street	B2	Heworth Green	A3	Ousegate	B2	The Mount	C1
Dalton Terrace	C1	Holgate Road	C1	Paragon Street	C2	The Stonebow	B2
Dodsworth Avenue	A3	Huntington Road	A3	Park Grove	A2	Tower Street	C2
				Penley's Grove Street	A2	Walmgate	B2
				Petergate	B2	Wigginton Road	A2

TOURIST INFORMATION ☎ 01904 620557
6 ROUGIER STREET, YORK, YO2 1JA

HOSPITAL A & E ☎ 01904 631313
YORK DISTRICT HOSPITAL, WIGGINTON ROAD,
YORK, Y31 8HE

COUNCIL OFFICE ☎ 01904 613161
THE GUILDHALL,
YORK, YO1 9QN

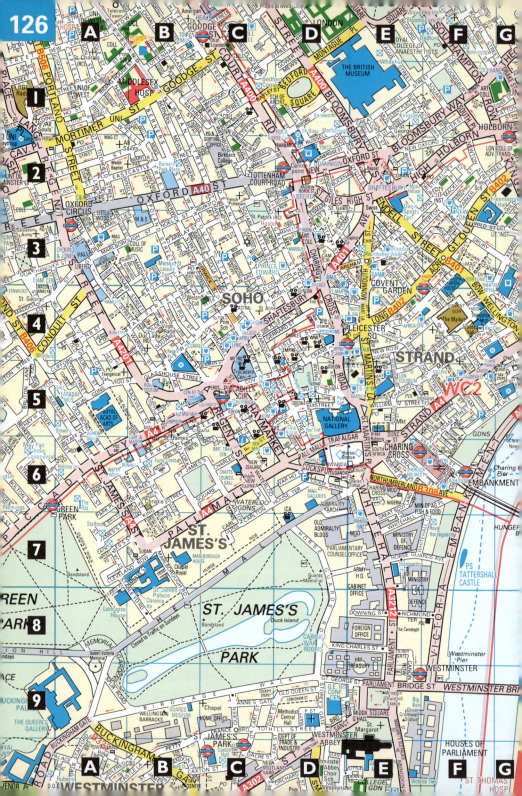

General Abbreviations

All.	Alley	Chyd.	Churchyard	Embk.	Embankment	Mkt.	Market	Sq.	Square
App.	Approach	Circ.	Circus	Est.	Estate	Mkts.	Markets	St.	Street,Saint
Arc.	Arcade	Clo.	Close	Gdn.	Garden	Ms.	Mews	Sta.	Station
Ave.	Avenue	Cor.	Corner	Gdns.	Gardens	Pas.	Passage	Ter.	Terrace
Bdy.	Broadway	Cres.	Crescent	Grd.	Ground	Pk.	Park	Twr.	Tower
Bldgs.	Buildings	Ct.	Court	Gro.	Grove	Pl.	Place	Wf.	Wharf
Bri.	Bridge	Ct.	Courtyard	Ho.	House	Rd.	Road	Wk.	Walk
Cen.	Centre,Central	E.	East	La.	Lane	Ri.	Rise	Yd.	Yard